EMPLOYMENT

by Cathy Fillmore Hoyt

LiteracyLink is a joint project of the PBS, Kentucky Educational Television, the National Center on Adult Literacy, and the Kentucky Department of Education. This project is funded in whole, or in part, by the Star Schools Program of the USDE under contract #R203D60001.

Acknowledgments

LiteracyLink® Advisory Board

Dr. Drew Albritton, American Association for Adult and Continuing Education

Peggy Barber, American Library Association

Anthony Buttino, WNED-TV

Dr. Anthony Carnevale, Educational Testing Service

Dr. Patricia Edwards, Michigan State University

Maggi Gaines, Baltimore Reads, Inc.

Dr. Milton Goldberg, National Alliance for Business

Columbus Hartwell, Exodus

Jan Hawkins, Center for Children and Technology, Education Development Corporation, Inc.

Neal Johnson, Educational Testing Service

Dr. Cynthia Johnston, Central Piedmont Community College

Thomas Kinney, American Association of Adult and Continuing Education

Dr. Jacqueline E. Korengel, Kentucky Department for Adult Ed and Literacy

Michael O'Brian, Certain Teed Corporation

Rafael Ramirez, U.S. Deptartment of Education

Dr. Emma Rhodes, Formerly of Arkansas Department of Education

Dr. Ahmed Sabie, Kentucky Department of Adult Education and Literacy

Tony Sarmiento, Worker Centered Learning, Working for America Institute

Dr. Steve Steurer, Correctional Education Association

Dr. Alice Tracy, Correctional Education Association

Dr. Fran Tracy-Mumford, Delaware Department of Adult/Community Education

Dr. Terilyn Turner, Community Education, St. Paul Public Schools

Dr. Renee Westcott, Central Piedmont Community College

Ex Officio Advisory Members

Joan Aucher, GED Testing Service

Cheryl Garnette, U.S. Department of Education

Dr. Andrew Hartman, National Institute for Literacy

Dr. Mary Lovell, U.S. Department of Education

Ronald Pugsley, U.S. Department of Education

Dr. Linda Roberts, U.S. Department of Education

Joe Wilkes, U.S. Department of Education

LiteracyLink Partners

LiteracyLink is a joint project of the Public Broadcasting Service, Kentucky Educational Television, the National Center on Adult Literacy, and the Kentucky Department of Education. This project is funded in whole, or in part, by the Star Schools Program of the USDE under contract #R203D60001.

Special thanks to the Kentucky Department for Adult Education and Literacy, Workforce Development Cabinet for its help on this project and for its vision and commitment to excellence in helping provide superior adult education products and services.

Workbook Production

Developer:
Learning Unlimited, Oak Park, Illinois

Design:
PiperStudios Inc., Chicago, Illinois

Cover Design and Layout:
By Design, Lexington, Kentucky

Project Consultant:
Milli Fazey, KET, Lexington, Kentucky

Production Manager:
Margaret Norman, KET, Lexington, Kentucky

ISBN 1-881020-34-7
ISBN 978-1-881020-34-9

Table of Contents

To the Teacher

The purpose of the *Workplace Essential Skills* series is to enable adult learners to become better informed and more highly skilled for the changing world of work. The materials are aimed at adults who are at the pre-GED (6th- to 8th-grade) reading level.

Twenty-four *Workplace Essential Skills* **television programs** model the application of basic skills within the context of pre-employment and workplace settings. The four accompanying **workbooks** present instruction, practice, and application of the critical skills that are represented in the programs:

- *Employment*
- *Communication & Wrtiting*
- *Reading*
- *Mathematics*

The series includes a utilization program for instructors and an overview program for learners.

The series also includes a **teacher's guide** for instructors and an **assessment instrument** to help learners and instructors determine the most effective course of study in the *Workplace Essential Skills* series.

Each lesson in the *Employment* workbook corresponds to one of the eight employability television programs in the *Workplace Essential Skills* series. The topics in the *Employment* workbook and the video programs are based on common labor market and workplace tasks.

Basic skills, problem solving, and decision making are integrated into every lesson. Additionally, interdisciplinary connections are inserted throughout the books for practice in real-world reading, writing, communication, math, and technology skills.

Taken together, the features and components of the *Workplace Essential Skills* instructional program provide a comprehensive grounding in the knowledge and skills learners need to succeed in the world of work. By also utilizing the ***LiteracyLink*** on-line component (see page vii), learners will begin to develop some of the computer literacy and Internet know-how needed to advance in the workplace of today and tomorrow.

Many of the skills covered in *Workplace Essential Skills* also provide a foundation for GED-level work in the areas of reading, math, and writing. Because high school completion is an important prerequisite for advancement in the work world, learners should be encouraged to go on to GED-level study when they are ready to do so. The ***LiteracyLink*** GED videos, print, and on-line materials (available in the year 2000) will provide an ideal context for learners to prepare for the GED tests and fulfill the requirement of high school equivalency.

To the Learner

Welcome to *Workplace Essential Skills: Employment.* This workbook has been designed to help you learn more about the ideas and skills presented in Programs 1–8 of the *Workplace Essential Skills* series. Take time to read about some of the features in this book.

1. The **Skills Preview** on pages 1–8 will help you discover which video programs and workbook lessons are most important for you. You can use the **Skills Preview Evaluation Chart** on page 10 to make your own personal study plan.

2. Each workbook lesson goes with a program in the television series. The lessons in this workbook cover Programs 1–8. Use the program number and title to find the corresponding tape and workbook lesson. After the opening page and **Objectives,** each lesson is divided into two parts:

   Before You Watch starts you thinking about the topics in the video program.

   - **Sneak Preview:** Exercise to preview some of the key concepts from the program.
   - **Answers for Sneak Preview:** Answers to the preview exercise.
   - **Feedback:** Information to help you personalize your work.
   - **Vocabulary:** Key terms from the lesson and their definitions.

   After You Watch allows you to apply skills that you saw in the program.

   - **Key Points from the Video Program:** List that summarizes the program.
   - **Situations:** Real-world problem solving from the health care, manufacturing, service, retail, and construction industries.
   - **Information:** In-depth information about important workplace concepts.
   - **WorkTips:** Hints for success in the world of work.
   - **WorkSkills:** Exercise that enables you to apply what you have learned.
   - **Connections:** Extension of workplace skills through practice in other content areas (*Write It, Tech Tip, Read It, Math Matters,* and *Communicate*).
   - **Review:** Section that lets you put all of your new workplace knowledge together.

3. The **Skills Review** allows you to evaluate what you have learned.

4. The **Answer Key** starts on page 165. There you can find answers to the exercises in each lesson, often with explanations, as well as samples of filled-in forms and documents.

5. The **Glossary,** which starts on page 175, includes key terms and definitions.

6. You can use the alphabetized **Index,** which starts on page 177, to look up information about employment issues.

7. A **Reference Handbook,** found on pages 179–184, is a helpful resource for you to access at any time. References to the handbook are listed throughout the book.

The LiteracyLink® System

Welcome to the *LiteracyLink* system. This workbook is one part of an educational system for adult learners and adult educators.

LiteracyLink consists of these learning tools:

Television programs
broadcast on
public television
and in adult
learning centers

Computer-based materials
available
through a
connection to the Internet

Workbooks
print-based
instruction
and practice

If you are working with *LiteracyLink* materials, you have a clear educational advantage. As you develop your knowledge and skills, you are also working with video and computer technology. This is the technology required to succeed in today's workplace, training programs, and colleges.

Content of the *LiteracyLink* System

The *LiteracyLink* system allows you to choose what you need to meet your goals. It consists of instruction and practice in the areas of:

Workplace Essential Skills
- Employment
  Pre-Employment and On-the-Job Skills
- Communication & Writing
  Listening, Speaking, and Writing Skills
- Reading
  Charts, Forms, Documents, and Manuals
- Mathematics
  Whole Numbers, Decimals, Fractions, and Percents

GED Preparation Series
- Language Arts Reading
  Fiction, Nonfiction, Poetry, Drama and Informational
- Language Arts Writing
  Essay Writing, Sentence Structure, Grammar, and Mechanics
- Social Studies
  U.S. History, World History, Geography, Civics and Government, and Economics
- Science
  Life Sciences, Earth and Space Sciences, Chemistry, and Physics
- Mathematics
  Arithmetic, Data Analysis, Algebra, and Geometry

Instructional Units

Units of study are used to organize *LiteracyLink's* instruction. For example, the first unit in this book is Planning to Work. To study this topic, you can use a video, workbook lesson, and computer. You will be able to easily find what you need since each workbook unit has the same title as a video and related Internet activities.

Getting Started With the System

It is possible to use each *LiteracyLink* component separately. However, you will make the best use of *LiteracyLink* if you use all of the parts. You can make this work in a way that is best for you through the *LiteracyLink* Internet site.

On the Internet site, you will take a Welcome Tour and establish your Home Space. The Home Space is your starting point for working through the online portion of *LiteracyLink*. It is also a place where you can save all of your online work.

An important part of the online system is LitHelper℠. This helps you to identify your strengths and weaknesses. LitHelper℠ helps you to develop an individualized study plan. The online LitLearner® materials, together with the videos and workbooks, provide hundreds of learning opportunities. Go to http://www.pbs.org/literacy to access the online material.

For Teachers

Parts of *LiteracyLink* have been developed for adult educators and service providers. LitTeacher® is an online professional development system. It provides a number of resources including PeerLit℠ a database of evaluated websites. At http://www.pbs.org/literacy you can also access *LitTeacher*.

Who's Responsible for *LiteracyLink*?

LiteracyLink was sparked by a five-year grant by the U.S. Department of Education. The following partners have contributed to the development of the *LiteracyLink* system:
- PBS Adult Learning Service
- Kentucky Educational Television (KET)
- The National Center on Adult Literacy (NCAL) of the University of Pennsylvania
- The Kentucky Department of Education

The *LiteracyLink* partners wish you the very best in achieving your educational goals.

Skills Preview

Questions 1–4 are based on the following situation.

CONSTRUCTION: Ned is learning more about different career paths and job openings. He needs to find a full-time job that will provide a steady income. Ned needs to earn at least $8 per hour to pay his bills. If possible, he would like to earn more so that he can put some money in savings. Ned needs a job with opportunities for advancement.

Ned prefers working outdoors. He likes to use tools and make things with his hands. Ned would like to get a job in construction, but he has no formal experience or training. Most of the jobs in the newspaper advertisements require at least one year of work experience.

1. Ned's neighbor tells him about a job opening as a helper at a car repair shop. What are some things Ned needs to find out to see whether the job will fit his needs? Check all that apply.

   _____ **a.** what the starting pay for the job is
   _____ **b.** whether he will like his co-workers
   _____ **c.** whether there will be a chance to move up in the company
   _____ **d.** whether the job is full-time or part-time

2. Ned finds out that the starting pay for the job at the car repair shop is $7.50 per hour, but Ned can get a raise of 30 cents per hour after he works there for six months. If earning $8 per hour immediately is the most important job requirement for Ned, he should

   (1) take the job until he can find a better-paying one
   (2) find a way to get by on less money
   (3) take the job and look for a second part-time job
   (4) look for another job that pays at least $8 per hour

3. Ned decides to interview someone in the construction field to gather information about that career field. To carry out a successful information interview, what should Ned do? Check all that apply.

   _____ **a.** Plan questions ahead of time to ask during the interview.
   _____ **b.** Dress as he would for a job interview.
   _____ **c.** Try to write down everything the person says.
   _____ **d.** Plan to take about an hour of the person's time.
   _____ **e.** Ask for suggestions of other people to interview.

4. What are two sources of information Ned can use to find out more about a career in construction? Write your answer on a separate piece of paper.

Questions 5–7 are based on the following situation.

SERVICE: Nicole likes working with animals. She has worked at a pet store where she helped customers find products for their pets. She also assisted the groomers and helped to exercise the dogs for sale at the pet store. Nicole has a dog of her own and has taken dog-training courses.

To find job leads, Nicole searches the want ads. She also visits a public career counseling service in her town to check the job postings. On Wednesday, she found the following posting on the bulletin board.

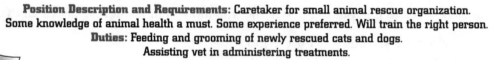

Job Services Office

For the position of: ANIMAL CARETAKER
Counselor: Alex Kapp • **Posting JOB# 3442541-4638**

Position Description and Requirements: Caretaker for small animal rescue organization. Some knowledge of animal health a must. Some experience preferred. Will train the right person.
Duties: Feeding and grooming of newly rescued cats and dogs.
Assisting vet in administering treatments.

Work: FULL-TIME • **Salary:** $7–$8 per hour
Hours: 7:30 A.M.–4:15 P.M. • **Days Off:** SUNDAY, MONDAY

5. Which of these is a true statement about Nicole's qualifications for this job?

   (1) Nicole does not have the necessary skills to apply for the job.
   (2) Nicole needs to take animal health classes to qualify for the job.
   (3) Many of the skills that Nicole acquired at the pet store can be transferred to the job as an animal caretaker.
   (4) The employer will not be interested in Nicole's experience with her own dog.

6. When Nicole talks to the Job Services counselor, she learns that the job has just been filled. Nicole decides to visit the animal rescue organization anyway. How could her visit help her find job leads? Check all that apply.

   _____ a. Nicole can expand her network of contacts.
   _____ b. Nicole can find out about the job's salary and benefits.
   _____ c. Nicole may find out about an unadvertised job opening.
   _____ d. Nicole can learn more about her chosen field of work.

7. When searching for job leads, why should Nicole read the entire want ads section from A to Z? Write your answer on a separate piece of paper.

Questions 8–12 are based on the following situation.

RETAIL: Jason heard about a job opening in sales at a software discount store. He has visited the store many times as a customer. Jason has a computer at home and understands how to decide whether software will run on a certain computer. He enjoys playing computer games and reading computer magazines.

Jason called the software store to find out how to apply for the job. The manager, Nancy Logan, told him to drop by the store to fill out a job application form.

Write *True* if the statement is true; *False* if it is false.

_____ 8. Jason probably will not have to fill out a job application form if he brings a resume to the store.

_____ 9. If a question on the job application form does not apply to Jason, he should leave the answer space blank.

10. Jason's job application form may be screened out, or rejected, for any of the following reasons. Check all that apply.

_____ **a.** messy writing
_____ **b.** answering open-ended questions in complete sentences
_____ **c.** not signing and dating the form
_____ **d.** untruthful answers
_____ **e.** not following directions

11. Jason worked as a salesperson at a department store last year for three months. He took the job to help pay his bills while he went back to school to learn more about computers. However, when the next school term started, he couldn't work out his school and work schedules, so he had to quit. What should Jason write in the space marked "Reason for Leaving Job"?

   (1) "I couldn't work out problems with my employer."
   (2) "I returned to school."
   (3) "I was laid off."
   (4) Jason should leave the space blank.

12. Near the end of the application form, Jason is asked, "Why do you want this job?" In his answer, Jason should

   (1) explain his financial needs
   (2) tell Nancy Logan a little about his family situation
   (3) talk more about his work-related strengths and skills
   (4) explain his long-range goals for school

Questions 13–18 are based on the following situation.

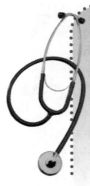

HEALTH CARE: Alicia is applying for a job as an information clerk at the county hospital. Her duties would involve greeting patients and visitors and giving them directions to help them find rooms and departments within the hospital.

Alicia finds out that the job at the hospital is full-time. It pays $360 per week and has good health benefits. But advancement opportunities at the hospital are few. To move up, Alicia would need to go back to school and take additional courses.

13. To apply for the job, Alicia will need to submit a resume. The resume should

   (1) include a paragraph explaining why she needs the job
   (2) describe her appearance
   (3) be at least two pages long
   (4) contain a summary of her work and educational experiences

Read these statements about writing resumes. Write *True* if the statement is true; *False* if it is false.

_____ 14. You should not include volunteer work on a resume.
_____ 15. As you describe your past work experiences, you should choose words that sound confident and positive.
_____ 16. If your resume contains errors, the employer may assume you are careless.

17. Alicia decides to list the pros and cons of taking the job at the hospital. Which of the following will Alicia list as a pro?

   (1) few advancement opportunities
   (2) more school required to move up
   (3) a long commute to and from work
   (4) good health benefits

18. Alicia has always wanted to work in a health care setting. She is excited about the job at the hospital, but she is concerned that the pay is too low for her needs. Alicia needs to earn about $30 more a week to pay her bills. If Alicia is offered the job at the hospital, she should

   (1) take the job and start looking immediately for one that pays more
   (2) take the job; then tell her employer she will have to quit unless she can earn more money
   (3) turn it down unless she can meet her financial needs another way
   (4) take the job and hope everything will work out okay

Questions 19–24 are based on the following situation.

SERVICE: Tony has a job interview with Esteban Ramos at A&B Tires. If he gets the job, Tony will be repairing and replacing tires on all kinds of vehicles. Tony hopes he can work his way up into a job in sales or management. Someday, he would like to own his own auto repair shop.

Tony is a strong, hard worker. He is eager to learn all about helping customers with their cars. After working for a few years, he would like to go back to school and learn more about car repair.

19. After inviting Tony into his office, Esteban says, "Tell me a little about yourself."
    Tony can best answer Esteban by talking about his

    (1) skills and work attitudes
    (2) family circumstances
    (3) personal life
    (4) financial status

20. Esteban asks Tony about his last job at Sportsland. He asks Tony what he liked least about working at the store. Actually, Tony had a hard time getting along with his supervisor, Mrs. Martin. Although Tony tried hard to make the changes in his work that Mrs. Martin suggested, she never seemed satisfied. To answer the interview question, Tony should

    (1) explain his feelings about Mrs. Martin to Esteban
    (2) pretend that he liked everything about the job
    (3) explain that he felt his skills would be better put to use in the automotive industry
    (4) tell Esteban that he was treated unfairly at Sportsland

Write *True* if the statement is true; *False* if it is false.

_____ 21. It would be illegal for Esteban to cite Tony's poor driving record as a reason not to hire Tony.

_____ 22. Tony should avoid making direct eye contact with Esteban during the interview.

_____ 23. Tony should not volunteer information that Esteban could use to discriminate against him.

24. Which of the following is a good question for Tony to ask the employer at the end of the interview?

    (1) "How long would I need to work here to earn vacation pay?"
    (2) "When will you be making a decision?"
    (3) "How many days of sick leave do I get each month?"
    (4) "Could you explain the health benefits that come with the job?"

Questions 25–28 are based on the following situation.

SERVICE: Lola has just been hired to work part-time at the public library. She works 12 noon to 6 P.M. on Monday through Friday. Her supervisor, Leon Grant, stresses that it is very important for her to be on time and put in a full day's work. During her shift, only three other workers in the small branch library are on duty. Lola thinks she will like the job. Her co-workers are friendly, and the work seems challenging.

25. On her first day, Lola is asked to put returned books back on the shelves. The system for nonfiction books seems difficult. Lola works alone for a few minutes, but thinks she is doing it wrong. Lola should

    (1) do something else until she can watch a co-worker do the task
    (2) ask her supervisor or a co-worker to explain the library system
    (3) work slowly until she figures out how the books are organized
    (4) do the best she can and blame any mistakes she might make on the unclear directions she was given

26. Lola gets a 15-minute break at 3 P.M. She needs to make an important phone call to her daughter's school at 2:30 P.M. Lola should

    (1) wait to call the school until 3:00
    (2) make the phone call at 2:30, then take her regular break on schedule
    (3) ask Leon for permission to take her break at 2:30
    (4) ask Leon for permission to take a longer break from 2:30 to 3:00

27. Which of the following expectations about new employees do employers have? Check all that apply.

    _____ **a.** come to work on time
    _____ **b.** treat the public with respect
    _____ **c.** solve problems without asking questions
    _____ **d.** be productive during the entire shift
    _____ **e.** learn the job by the end of the first day
    _____ **f.** work well with their co-workers

28. Leon tells Lola that tomorrow he will begin teaching her how to use the library's computer tracking system. Lola has never used a computer. She is so worried that she won't do well that she feels like quitting. Lola should

    (1) look for another job that doesn't involve computers
    (2) tell her supervisor that she doesn't want to learn the system
    (3) take this opportunity to develop her work skills
    (4) pretend that she already understands how to use the tracking system

Questions 29–34 are based on the following situation.

RETAIL: Rico works for a home improvement store. Today he is unpacking mirrors for display in the store. His supervisor gave him a solvent, or cleaning fluid, to use to remove any stickers and tags from the glass surfaces. The warning label for the solvent is shown below.

> **ALWAYS USE SAFETY GOGGLES. FOR PROLONGED USE, WEAR SOLVENT-RESISTANT GLOVES.**
>
> **DANGER! FLAMMABLE.** KEEP AWAY FROM HEAT, SPARKS, FLAME, AND ELECTRICITY. USE ONLY WITH ADEQUATE VENTILATION. STOP USE IMMEDIATELY IF YOU EXPERIENCE DIZZINESS, HEADACHES, NAUSEA, OR EYE WATERING. IN CASE OF INGESTION OR EYE CONTACT, CALL PHYSICIAN IMMEDIATELY.

29. Rico has never used this solvent before. What would his employer expect him to do in this situation? Check all that apply.

____ **a.** read the directions carefully
____ **b.** refrain from using the product
____ **c.** wear safety goggles and gloves
____ **d.** ask the supervisor what safety equipment he should use
____ **e.** use common sense in choosing a safe place to do the work

30. While using the solvent, Rico spills a small amount on the floor of a store aisle. The odor from the spill is strong. Rico's first concern should be to

    (1) stop working and leave the area
    (2) make sure no one is in danger because of the hazard
    (3) clean up the spill
    (4) make a sign to warn people about the spill

Write *True* if the statement is true; *False* if it is false.

_____ 31. Rico's employer is legally responsible for training employees to work safely.
_____ 32. Every new piece of equipment at a workplace such as Rico's comes with a manual that explains how to operate the machine safely.
_____ 33. Rico's employer should not expect him to follow every safety procedure, only the most important ones.

34. If Rico does not have safety goggles or gloves, he should

    (1) discuss the problem with his supervisor
    (2) display the mirrors without removing the labels
    (3) use the solvent very carefully
    (4) try to remove the labels some other way

Questions 35–40 are based on the following situation.

RETAIL: Shelly was recently hired to work at a video rental store. To help her learn the job, her supervisor, Nelson, gives her an employee handbook. He also assigns Rick, a co-worker, to train her.

Rick first teaches Shelly how to work the register. She learns to ask customers for their store membership card and run it through the scanner. Then she makes sure the rented video matches the computer printout. Finally, she collects payment.

35. A customer wants to rent a video, but he doesn't have his store membership card with him. Shelly hasn't been taught what to do in this situation. A long line of customers waits. Shelly should

    (1) go ahead and rent the video to the customer
    (2) tell the customer that she is new and ask him to go to another line
    (3) take time to look up the problem in the employee handbook
    (4) ask a co-worker for help

36. Shelly wants to learn more about the other jobs done at the store because she hopes to move up in the company and become a store manager. Unfortunately, Nelson and Rick have little time to train her. What are some things Shelly can do to take responsibility for her own learning? Check all that apply.

    ____ **a.** observe co-workers doing their jobs
    ____ **b.** give suggestions to co-workers for better ways to do their jobs
    ____ **c.** sign up for any formal training courses offered by the company
    ____ **d.** read the employee handbook

Write *True* if the statement is true; *False* if it is false.

_____ 37. To improve her learning, Shelly should practice the skills she is taught as soon as possible.

_____ 38. A job review is a chance for Shelly to set goals to improve her work.

_____ 39. Workers often receive very low scores on the first job review.

40. At the end of the first week, Nelson compliments Shelly on her good work. Then he asks her to work a little faster when she reshelves the videos. Shelly feels angry about the criticism because she feels the other workers leave most of the reshelving work for her. Shelly should

    (1) complain to Nelson about other workers not doing their fair share
    (2) point out politely that reshelving videos is not her only job duty
    (3) accept the suggestion and try to reshelve the videos a little faster
    (4) explain that it is not her fault that the reshelving is taking so long

Skills Preview Answer Key

1. a, c, d
2. (4) look for another job that pays at least $8 per hour
3. a, b, e
4. Any two of the following: family, friends, information interviews, a career counseling service, the library, the Internet
5. (3) Many of the skills that Nicole acquired at the pet store can be transferred to the job as an animal caretaker.
6. a, c, d
7. The want ads are organized by key words, and employers may place an ad under any one of a variety of key words. Note that some words may not be obvious key words.
8. False
9. False
10. a, c, d, e
11. (2) "I returned to school."
12. (3) talk more about his work-related strengths and skills
13. (4) contain a summary of her work and educational experiences
14. False
15. True
16. True
17. (4) good health benefits
18. (3) turn it down unless she can meet her financial needs another way
19. (1) skills and work attitudes
20. (3) explain that he felt his skills would be better put to use in the automotive industry
21. False
22. False
23. True
24. (2) "When will you be making a decision?"
25. (2) ask her supervisor or a co-worker to explain the library system
26. (3) ask Leon for permission to take her break at 2:30
27. a, b, d, f
28. (3) take this opportunity to develop her work skills
29. a, c, e
30. (2) make sure no one is in danger because of the hazard
31. True
32. True
33. False
34. (1) discuss the problem with his supervisor
35. (4) ask a co-worker for help
36. a, c, d
37. True
38. True
39. False
40. (3) accept the suggestion and try to reshelve the videos a little faster

Skills Preview Evaluation Chart

Circle the question numbers that you answered correctly. Then fill in the number of questions you got correct for each program lesson. Find the total number correct, and focus your work on the lessons you had trouble with.

Program Lesson	Question Number	Number Correct/Total
1: *Planning to Work* Thinking About Work, Making a Career Plan, Researching Jobs and Careers	1, 2, 3, 4	____/4
2: *Matching Skills and Jobs* Assessing Your Employability, Finding Job Leads, Making the Job Search Your Job	5, 6, 7	____/3
3: *Applying for Jobs* Figuring Out the Application Process, Learning How Employers Screen Job Seekers, Completing Job Application Forms	8, 9, 10, 11, 12	____/5
4: *Resumes, Tests, and Choices* Understanding the Purposes of Resumes, Deciding Which Job Openings to Pursue, Comparing Job Opportunities	13, 14, 15, 16, 17, 18	____/6
5: *Interviewing* Exploring the Interview Process, Preparing for an Interview, Interviewing and Follow-up	19, 20, 21, 22, 23, 24	____/6
6: *Ready for Work* Understanding Your Employer's Expectations, Learning the Meaning of "Work-Ready," Working as a New Hire	25, 26, 27, 28	____/4
7: *Workplace Safety* Understanding Safety Issues, Recognizing Safety Issues, Learning How to Protect Yourself and Your Co-workers	29, 30, 31, 32, 33, 34	____/6
8: *Learning at Work* Learning on the Job, Taking Charge of Your Own Training, Training over the Long Term	35, 36, 37, 38, 39, 40	____/6
	Total	____/40

WHAT YOUR SCORE MEANS

If you got 36–40 correct: You have a good understanding of how to find job leads, represent your skills and strengths, and communicate well with co-workers, supervisors, and employers.

If you got 32–35 correct: You have a basic knowledge of how to pursue job leads and learn a new job. You may need to improve your understanding of how to work to your potential on the job.

If you got 28–31 correct: Through study and practice, you can improve your knowledge in some skills areas. As you improve your knowledge base, you will be better prepared to meet your future employer's expectations.

If you got fewer than 28 correct: You need to learn more about how to be successful in the job hunt and on the job. By watching the video programs and doing the exercises in this book, you can gain the knowledge and skills you need.

Planning to Work

The video program you are about to watch shows some of the reasons people enter the workplace. The program will help you get a sense of what kind of **job** you are interested in and how to gather information about that job from many sources.

As you watch, think about the kinds of **careers** that could bring you both money and satisfaction. You will be happier in a job if your financial needs are met and you feel pride in your accomplishments.

Once you have chosen a career direction, you will need to gather information to focus your thinking. There are many sources available to you, from people you know to library books to **on-line** services. Keep the information in a notebook or folder. Information you gather will help you choose the best job for you.

Sneak Preview

This exercise previews some of the concepts from Program 1. After you answer the questions, use the Feedback on page 13 to help set your learning goals.

SERVICE: Ruben is a high school graduate who wants a career in business. Right now, he needs a full-time job to pay for classes at the community college and to help out his family. He types 30 words per minute and uses computers in school. Ruben has been researching career paths that involve office work. In a job handbook at the library, Ruben finds this job description:

OFFICE CLERK

NATURE OF WORK
- Office clerks perform a variety of duties depending on the needs of their employers.
- They may file or type, enter data on a computer, process mail, and answer telephones.
- They may be asked to operate photocopiers, fax machines, and other kinds of office equipment.

WORKING CONDITIONS
- Office clerks generally work a regular 40-hour week.
- There may be some overtime work and opportunities for temporary work.

TRAINING AND QUALIFICATIONS
- The job of office clerk is usually an entry-level job.
- Most employers require a high school diploma, typing skills, and some computer experience.
- Because office clerks often assist the public, they need good communication skills.
- They also need to be cooperative and work well with other members of the office staff.
- Office clerks with good skills may be promoted to supervisor positions in business administration.

EARNINGS
- Experienced, full-time office clerks earn between $15,000 and $25,000 per year.
- A beginning office clerk earns between $11,500 and $13,000.

Answer these questions based on the situation described above.

1. Ruben needs to earn at least $14,500 per year. If earning this salary level is the most important reason for Ruben to work, should he look for a job as an office clerk? Explain your thinking.

   _____

   _____

2. What are three reasons why the job of office clerk may be a good choice for Ruben? Check the three that apply.

   _____ **a.** The job of office clerk is related to Ruben's career path.
   _____ **b.** Ruben could work in the evenings if he wanted to.
   _____ **c.** Ruben can meet the requirements of the job.
   _____ **d.** Ruben could learn more about using computers.

3. Ruben has prepared a list of questions to learn more about working as an office clerk. Which of his questions can be answered by the information Ruben found in the job handbook? Check all that apply.

____ **a.** What specific employers in my area hire office clerks?

____ **b.** What responsibilities does an office clerk have?

____ **c.** Are there any opportunities for advancement?

____ **d.** Will more office clerks be needed in the future?

____ **e.** How much money can I expect to earn starting out?

4. How could Ruben learn more about working in an office? List three sources of information.

_____

_____

_____

Feedback

- If you got all of the answers right...   you have a foundation for gathering information about a career path. As you watch the video program, think about what career might best meet your needs, interest you, and allow you to use your skills.

- If you missed question 1 ...   you need to think more about the reasons people work.

- If you missed question 2 ...   you need to learn more about how jobs and careers are related.

- If you missed question 3 ...   you need to think about how you can use the information you gather to answer questions about your career path.

- If you missed question 4 ...   you need to explore what resources are available to provide information about jobs and careers.

Vocabulary for *Planning to Work*

benefits	employee sick leave, vacation, and insurance assistance that is paid by the company
careers	job positions for which a person plans and trains
career path	a carefully chosen series of jobs within a given profession. A career path usually begins with an entry-level job in a profession. Over time, as an employee gains more knowledge and experience, the career path will include jobs involving more responsibilities and higher pay.
challenges	tasks that test the limits of a worker's skills and knowledge
consumer	someone who buys goods and services
counselor	someone who is trained to give advice about a particular subject
economy	the financial health of a city, state, or country
fixed expenses	amounts that a person knows he or she will have to spend each month
goals	end points a person wants to reach
interest	the cost of borrowing money
Internet	a worldwide group of computer networks that have been linked together
job	a duty performed regularly by an employee for a specified wage, or payment
on-line	being connected to a computer network
outlook	what to expect in the future
priorities	goals put in order according to their importance
standard of living	a level of comfort measured by what a person owns and earns
vocational colleges	schools that teach practical skills in certain trades

PBS LiteracyLink®

Now watch Program 1.

After you watch, work on:
- pages 15–28 in this workbook
- Internet activities at www.pbs.org/literacy

AFTER you WATCH

program **1**

Planning to Work

On the following pages, you will learn more about the ideas discussed in the video program and have an opportunity to develop and practice your skills.

Think About the Key Points from the Video Program

To get ready to work, you need to:
- Think about your needs and how much money you must earn to pay for these needs.
- Think about what kind of work gives you personal satisfaction.
- Think about what kind of work matches your interests, skills, and talents.

After you are ready to work, you should make a career plan. To do so, you need to:
- Gather information about your career from many sources.
- Use city and county job services.
- Find out about training programs and schools in your area.

Once you have chosen a job or career plan, you are ready to gather research. To do so, you need to:
- Decide what questions you need answered about your career choice.
- Use the library, on-line resources, and people you know to find the answers.
- Use your research as you set goals to help you achieve success in your career.

Thinking About Work

SERVICE: Your friend Bonita loves gardening. She has been earning some money taking care of people's yards, but she needs to earn more. Now she is looking for a full-time job with **benefits.** She had planned to research and look for a job in landscaping, but her brother can get her a job at the bank where he works. The job has benefits but would pay barely enough money to cover Bonita's bills. **Should Bonita take the bank job? Explain your thinking.**

_____

_____

_____

Money is important to everyone. You need it to pay for shelter, food, and clothing, but you also need money to pay for your wants. Maybe you want to go back to school, take a vacation, give your child music lessons, or start a new hobby. Whatever your dreams and desires are, you will probably need money to accomplish them.

Finding out more about your needs and wants can help you find a job that offers the financial security you need.

Know Your Basic Needs

Look at the money you spend each month. Estimate how much money goes to necessities—those things you need to live. Did you include items like groceries, rent, utilities, and clothing? Do you have credit card bills or loan payments? Do you have transportation or child-care expenses? Will these expenses increase when you start to work? If so, estimate what they will be when you start to work.

The total of these **fixed expenses** is the minimum amount of money you need to earn each month. If you decide to take a job that pays less than this amount, you will need either to reduce your expenses or meet them in some other way.

Pay Off Your Debts

At times, you may have borrowed money to pay for your needs and wants. Most loans require you to pay **interest.** Paying interest takes away from the money you have available to pay your bills and meet your goals. If you are in debt, one important reason to work is to get out of debt. By paying just a little more than the minimum amount due on your loans, you will soon have more money available to improve your **standard of living.**

Save for the Future

One reason to work is to save money. Setting aside a little money each paycheck is important, even if the amount is small. There are good reasons to save.

Your savings can help out in an emergency. Unexpected car repairs or a doctor bill can cause stress if you don't know how you can find the money to pay for it. If you stick to your plan of saving a little each month, your savings will be there to help.

Your savings is also an investment in your future. You may want to go back to school, get a bigger place to live, buy a car, or take a vacation. Your savings can help make your dreams possible.

WORKTIP

As you begin your job search:

- Don't rush. Give yourself time to find the right job.
- Don't take a job you don't like just because a friend thinks it's a good idea.
- Expect highs and lows. Thinking about a new job is exciting, but it can also seem overwhelming. Both feelings are normal.

WorkSkills

1. You need to earn at least enough to cover your fixed expenses. Which of these are fixed expenses? Check all that apply.

    ____ **a.** the cost of a bus pass for someone who takes the bus
    ____ **b.** bills for electricity and water
    ____ **c.** the cost of basic phone service
    ____ **d.** the cost of movie tickets
    ____ **e.** monthly rent
    ____ **f.** a restaurant bill
    ____ **g.** a loan payment
    ____ **h.** the cost of a magazine

2. Bonita has decided not to take the job at the bank. She thinks the pay at the bank is too low, but she isn't sure. She asks for your help in figuring out how much she really needs to earn each month. What information does she need to know about her spending habits? What would you say to her? Write your reply to her on the lines below or on a separate piece of paper.

    _____

    _____

    _____

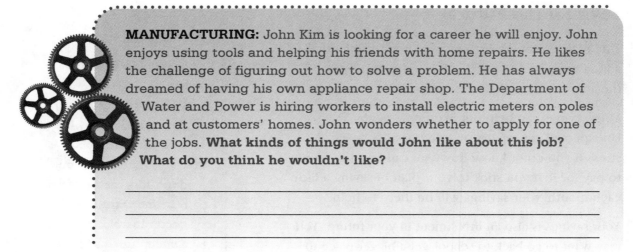

MANUFACTURING: John Kim is looking for a career he will enjoy. John enjoys using tools and helping his friends with home repairs. He likes the challenge of figuring out how to solve a problem. He has always dreamed of having his own appliance repair shop. The Department of Water and Power is hiring workers to install electric meters on poles and at customers' homes. John wonders whether to apply for one of the jobs. **What kinds of things would John like about this job? What do you think he wouldn't like?**

_____

_____

_____

How can you tell when a career is right for you? You bring a special set of talents, interests, and needs to the workplace. If you find your job interesting and you are using your talents, you are likely to be happy in your job. Earning money is important. Getting satisfaction from a job well done is important too.

Feel Proud of Your Accomplishments

Think about something you have done that has given you pride in yourself. Chances are whatever you accomplished was brought about by hard work. People are proud when they solve a difficult problem or make a difference in someone else's life or their community. You are more likely to be successful in your job and enjoy work if you are accomplishing something you see as important.

Find the Right Amount of Challenge

Every job presents **challenges.** Some challenges are physical. You may need to move, bend, lift, and carry. You may be on your feet for hours at a time. To overcome these challenges, you need strength and stamina.

Some challenges are mental. You may be asked to make decisions about the best way to do a job or the next step to take to get the work done.

Some challenges are social. You will need to be polite and fair as you greet the public and work with supervisors and fellow workers.

Finding a job with the right amount and right kinds of challenges will help you find satisfaction in your work. **In your notebook or on a separate piece of paper, list the kinds of challenges you look forward to facing on the job.**

Find Your Role in the Community

As a **consumer,** you encourage growth in business and industry as you earn and spend money. When companies grow, they employ more workers, strengthening the community in which they do business. Your consumer dollars help to keep the **economy** healthy. While planning how you spend your earnings, keep in mind that your dollars affect a large community of people.

. . . .

WorkSkills

1. What are two reasons to work besides to earn money?

   _____

   _____

2. Imagine what it would be like to be a clerk in a grocery store. List two examples of social challenges you may encounter.

   _____

   _____

3. Suppose John Kim takes the job at the Department of Water and Power. Which of the following is a mental challenge he may face?

   (1) communicating with his supervisor
   (2) climbing a utility pole
   (3) figuring out why a meter does not work
   (4) driving a repair truck

WRITE IT

As you work and gain more purchasing power, your purchases will have a greater influence on the economy. Try this exercise to see the impact of your shopping decisions.

- On a separate piece of paper, list five products or services that you purchase regularly.
- For each product or service, list all the jobs and businesses that are affected by your purchase.

For example, a purchase of disposable diapers affects workers at companies that make diapers, paper, and plastic. It affects advertising jobs. It also affects store jobs such as stock clerk, cashier, grocery bagger, and so on.

Making a Career Plan

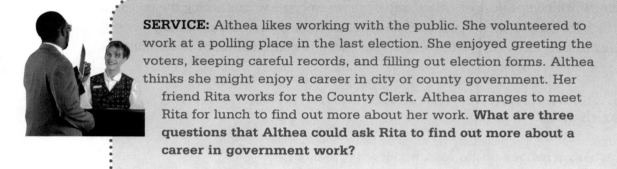

SERVICE: Althea likes working with the public. She volunteered to work at a polling place in the last election. She enjoyed greeting the voters, keeping careful records, and filling out election forms. Althea thinks she might enjoy a career in city or county government. Her friend Rita works for the County Clerk. Althea arranges to meet Rita for lunch to find out more about her work. **What are three questions that Althea could ask Rita to find out more about a career in government work?**

_____

_____

_____

A career is much more than a job. Your career is your life's work. Your **career path** is the course you will follow to try to achieve your work-related goals.

Career planning is a process. You need to gather information about yourself and your talents and interests. You also need to know what skills and training might be necessary to succeed in a career. Then you need to analyze the information you have gathered to make good decisions.

Choosing a career requires planning and thought. There are many sources of information that can help you find the answers to questions you may have.

Gather Information from Friends and Family

The best place to find information about a new career may be your own home. Ask your family, friends, and neighbors to tell you what they know about the career path you are considering. Perhaps some have held jobs in your desired field of work or know someone who has. Perhaps they have had experiences with workers in your chosen field.

Ask them about the kind of job duties you may have. Find out what they know about the kind of skills and training you will need to succeed on the job.

Most important, your family and friends know you. They know your strengths and your weaknesses. They can help you set and achieve personal goals that will help you succeed in your career.

Use Community Resources

Talk about your career interests with everyone you meet. You never know who will be able to help. Don't suppose that people know only the jobs they are doing. They work with other people who hold different jobs at their workplace. They probably have some knowledge of the job duties these people perform.

Another source of information is the public library. Ask the librarian to help you locate books, magazines, and newspaper articles about your area of interest. The librarian can show you how to use an index arranged by subject to find specific magazine articles. If a book or magazine article is not available at your library, the librarian may be able to order it for you. Many libraries also offer **Internet** services you can use to search for information. You may be able to go on line to interview someone working in your field of interest.

WORKTIP

As you gather information:

- Be patient. You can't learn everything there is to know in one day. Take it one step at a time.
- Stay organized. Use note cards to record what you have learned. On each card, put the date and the name of the person who gave you the information.
- Keep going. Do at least one thing every day to help yourself achieve your career goals.

WorkSkills

1. How could you find out more about a career that interests you? List four sources of information.

   _____   _____

   _____   _____

2. Suppose you wanted to get a job as a cook at a restaurant. What other workers at the restaurant might know something about the cook's job? List at least three.

   _____   _____

   _____   _____

Write *True* if the statement is true; *False* if it is false.

_____ 3. You can use the Internet to gather information about a career.

_____ 4. The best way to find magazine articles about your career is to thumb through every magazine on the shelf.

_____ 5. If you want to be a nurse, talking with nurse's aides is probably a waste of your time.

MANUFACTURING: Karina has always been interested in machines. She enjoys figuring out how things work, studying diagrams, and using tools. Karina would like to work as an industrial mechanic, someone who maintains and repairs equipment in a factory. She lives near a manufacturing plant where her father works as a packer. He says that she could start out as a mechanic's helper at the plant. Karina isn't sure whether she should try to get a job as a helper and work her way up or go back to school. **What are some ways Karina could gather more information about the best way to enter this career field?**

_____

_____

Use Career Counseling Services

Most communities have services that can help you gather information about your career path. Your city or county may have public services that are available at no cost to you. To find out more about these services, look under the heading *Government* in your telephone book. Find the heading *Employment* under the city, county, and state government sections.

Find the Job Services Department, which is usually a part of the Employment Development Department. Job Services can help you find out more about the **outlook** for jobs in your career field, the skills and qualifications that you will need for your career, and the amount you could expect to earn. Call the office number listed in the telephone book and make an appointment. An experienced **counselor** will help you gather more information about your career.

Explore Training Programs

You will likely need more training to move up the career ladder. You may be able to get on-the-job training in which a more experienced employee trains you, supervises you, and checks your work carefully. If you are required to have a certificate, license, or degree to hold a particular job, you may need to go back to school.

Community, technical, and **vocational colleges** all prepare people to work in specific careers. Ask the admissions office of each school about the cost of the program or classes you must take. Ask what percentage of students finish the program once they begin it. You should also ask what percentage of students who finish the program get jobs. High percentages in both categories are best.

Look at Financial Aid Options

To pay for more training, you may qualify for grants or loans. *Grants* are a type of financial aid that you don't have to pay back. *Loans* are borrowed money that you must repay, usually with interest. Work-study is another kind of financial assistance. In a work-study program, you work at the school you attend. For more information, talk to a financial aid officer at your school.

WorkSkills

1. Milan is interested in a career in the health field as a laboratory technician. Which of these facts could he find out from a career counseling service? Check all that apply.

   _____ a. the amount he could expect to earn as a laboratory technician
   _____ b. the kinds of financial aid he could receive to go back to school
   _____ c. the number of expected future job openings for laboratory technicians
   _____ d. the need to earn a special certificate or license to be a laboratory technician

Write *True* if the statement is true; *False* if it is false.

_____ 2. On-the-job training is usually provided at a high school.
_____ 3. You may need to take classes to get a certificate or license.
_____ 4. Vocational and technical colleges don't track the number of their students who get jobs.

5. Compare and contrast grants and loans. How are they the same? How are they different?

   _____

   _____

TECH TIP

The Internet can be a tool for researching your career. Just type in a key word or phrase, and the computer will search for items that match your request.

Specific key words and phrases are better than general ones. For example, the word *job* would result in too many matches to be useful, but the phrase *job opportunities in carpentry* might be just right. If one search doesn't lead to the information you want, try another. **On a separate piece of paper, make a list of five phrases that you could use in an Internet search to find information about your career path.**

Researching Jobs and Careers

SERVICE: Tanya Morris has always wanted to work in law enforcement. After reading the want ads in the classified section of the newspaper, she feels confused and frustrated because there are so many different job titles in her career field. Tanya wonders how she can get more information about each job title. **What are some things Tanya could do to get the information she needs?**

_____

_____

_____

Conduct Information Interviews

For specific information about a career, you may need to talk to someone who works in the field in which you are interested. In an information interview, you are there to gather information, not to ask for a job.

Find the name of someone who has the kind of job you would like to have. Ask your friends and family members for ideas. Call the employee and make an appointment. Promise to take no more than fifteen minutes of his or her time.

When you go to the appointment, dress as you would for a job interview. Be prepared with at least six questions that you could ask. Be prepared to write down important facts. Be respectful of this person's time. Do not take more than the fifteen minutes you requested unless the person volunteers to talk longer. After the interview, write a short letter thanking the worker for his or her time and help.

Ask Good Questions

Whether you are conducting an information interview, meeting with a career services counselor, or talking to family and friends, you need to know the right questions to ask. Even when you are reading about your career, you need to have good questions in mind so that you will know what information is important to write down and remember. **Use the following lists to write questions of your own on a separate piece of paper.**

Good Questions for a Job Research Situation

- What job titles are associated with my career?
- What are the duties for each job title?
- What are the training and education requirements for this career?
- What educational opportunities are there in my community to receive this training?
- How much could I expect to earn as an entry-level worker? How much could I earn with experience?
- What is the employment outlook for this career?
- What are the common ways to advance in this career field?

Good Questions for an Information Interview

- Why did you choose your career?
- What is your job title? Are there other titles for your job?
- What training and education did you need to do your job?
- What are the most important tasks of this job?
- What do you like best about your job?
- Do you have any advice for someone interested in this career?
- Is there anyone else whom I should talk to?

WorkSkills

1. Check all the things you *should* do related to information interviews.

   _____ **a.** Plan what questions you will ask before the interview.
   _____ **b.** During the interview, write down everything that is said.
   _____ **c.** Find out information about a specific job.
   _____ **d.** Expect the interview to last about an hour.
   _____ **e.** Write a thank-you letter to the person you interviewed.

2. Suppose you want to work as a retail clerk at a certain department store. What would be the best way to find out more about the specific job duties?

   (1) Visit a career counseling service.
   (2) Talk to a store employee who works as a retail clerk.
   (3) Ask your family and friends.
   (4) Look it up at the library.

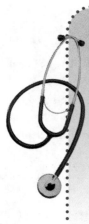

HEALTH CARE: Mark Cook wants to become a dental hygienist. His research shows that he could earn over $40,000 a year if he works hard. It also shows he would need to go back to school to get an associate's degree and pass a test to get his license. Mark doesn't see how he can go back to school now. He needs a car and his family wants a bigger apartment. He needs to get a job now. **How could setting goals help Mark accomplish his career plan?**

_____

_____

_____

Use the Information You Have Gathered

By now, you have had the opportunity to gather a good deal of information about the world of work and your field of interest. Now you need to use all this information to set goals and make a plan of action.

Set Goals

Having **goals** is the key to staying on track and ending up where you want to in your life.

A *long-term goal* is the end result. Completing a degree, getting married, and buying a car are some examples of long-term goals. People who have long-term goals are much more likely to reach their potential, or full ability, than those who don't.

Short-term goals are the steps you must complete to reach a long-term goal. If your long-term goal is buying a car, your short-term goals may be researching makes and models of cars, examining your finances, deciding where to buy the car, and making a deal for the car you want.

Make a Plan of Action

Take a look at Mark Cook's plan of action for becoming a dental hygienist.

Goal	Become a dental hygienist
Step 1	Work with family to set **priorities.**
Step 2	Get a full-time job as a dental assistant or receptionist.
Step 3	Take night classes to complete an associate's degree.
Step 4	Pass test for dental hygienist's license.

As you can see, Mark's short-term goals become his plan of action. Think about your long-term career goal. What steps will you need to accomplish first? **Write a plan of action for your long-term career goal.**

You may need to change or add some steps as you begin to follow your plan of action. Don't worry about it. Your plan of action belongs to you. It is a tool for helping you acquire the future you have chosen.

WorkSkills

1. Jan wants to be an elementary school teacher someday. Which of the following are steps that could bring her closer to this goal? Check all that apply.

    _____ a. Work part-time as a teacher's aide.

    _____ b. Make an appointment with a college counselor to find out what classes she needs to take.

    _____ c. Take an accounting class.

    _____ d. Learn to speak Spanish, a language spoken by many children in her community.

    _____ e. Work full-time as an order filler for a catalog company.

    _____ f. Coach a soccer team of eight-year-olds.

Write *True* if the statement is true; *False* if it is false.

_____ 2. A plan of action should not be changed.

_____ 3. Short-term goals are the steps you must complete to achieve your long-term goal.

_____ 4. You should decide upon a plan of action before you set a long-term goal.

5. Your friend Ron needs a job. He isn't sure what kind of career he would like to have. Why would it be a good idea for Ron to do some research and set a long-term goal before he takes a job?

_____

_____

WRITE IT

Review the information you have gathered about your field of interest. **Based on your research, write one or two paragraphs in your notebook or on a separate piece of paper describing the job you would most like to have. Include the job title, its duties and responsibilities, and any special training or education you would need.**

Review

CONSTRUCTION: Marilyn is researching different career paths and current job openings. She wants to have a steady income that she can count on. She's tired of having to decide which bills she can pay one month and which bills need to wait until next month. She also wants to quit jumping from job to job.

Marilyn saw an advertisement for a sales job that lets a person work out of his or her home. The listed potential salary is high, and the hours are flexible. The job would involve a lot of phone work, but she could start immediately.

While looking at different training programs, Marilyn discovers that if she gets a job as an apprentice with a labor union, they would train her to become a journeyman. As an apprentice, the pay wouldn't be that great, and she would have to pay union dues. But after she completes her training and apprenticeship, the union would help place her in jobs as a journeyman. The union has a very good pay scale and health insurance package.

1. Look at the following list. Check the *five* most important things Marilyn should think about when choosing the job that will lead to a career.

   _____ **a.** starting salary
   _____ **b.** room for advancement or promotion
   _____ **c.** training requirements
   _____ **d.** job security
   _____ **e.** number of vacation days
   _____ **f.** health insurance and other benefits
   _____ **g.** steady work and regular hours

2. If Marilyn focuses only on her immediate need to pay bills, which job do you think she will apply for? Explain your reasoning.

   _____

   _____

   _____

3. Marilyn needs to do some research to make a good career decision. List three ways in which Marilyn can learn more about her career options.

   _____

   _____

   _____

BEFORE you WATCH

program **2**

WATCH

Matching Skills and Jobs

The video program you are about to watch shows some of the ways people find out about job openings. The program will help you prepare to gather information about job leads in person and over the telephone. You will also see how the classified ads and job postings can help you find out about job openings.

As you talk to employers about jobs, they will want to know more about you. They will be interested in how your skills and experiences could help them on the job. As you watch the video, think about the personal qualities you have that will make you a good employee. Think about your skills, talents, and interests. How can you use them on the job? Think about your work experience—both paid and unpaid. How can your experiences make you a better worker?

Successful job seekers treat the job search like a job. Plan to spend several hours a day preparing yourself, talking with people about job openings, visiting workplaces, and checking the want ads and other job postings. Keep all information in your job notebook or folder. Practice your work skills as you work to get a job and you will soon find a job that meets your needs.

OBJECTIVES

In this lesson, you will work with the following concepts and skills:

1. Assessing your skills, experiences, and interests
2. Using want ads and job postings to find out about available jobs
3. Making the job search your job

Sneak Preview

This exercise previews some of the concepts from Program 2. After you answer the questions, use the Feedback on page 31 to help set your learning goals.

SERVICE: Marisol has been looking for a job for three weeks. She worked as a food server at a local restaurant for four months, but she would prefer to work in an office. So far, Marisol's only job-search strategy has been reading the want ads. Each day she reads the classified ads listed under *Office.* One day she finds the following ad in the paper. After reading it, she uses the library fax machine to send her resume to apply for the job.

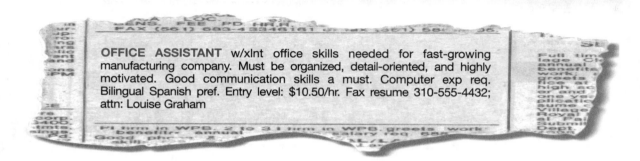

OFFICE ASSISTANT w/xlnt office skills needed for fast-growing manufacturing company. Must be organized, detail-oriented, and highly motivated. Good communication skills a must. Computer exp req. Bilingual Spanish pref. Entry level: $10.50/hr. Fax resume 310-555-4432; attn: Louise Graham

Answer these questions based on the situation described above.

1. According to the ad, which skills are *required?* Check all that apply.

     _____ **a.** good communication skills
     _____ **b.** typing at 50 wpm
     _____ **c.** computer skills
     _____ **d.** high motivation
     _____ **e.** previous work experience
     _____ **f.** skill in organizing work
     _____ **g.** ability to speak Spanish

Write *True* if the statement is true; *False* if it is false.

_____ 2. Marisol will be able to locate a job as an office assistant only through the want ads.

_____ 3. Employers looking for office workers will not be interested in hearing about Marisol's job as a food server.

_____ 4. Marisol could use examples from her experiences as a food server to demonstrate that she has good communication skills.

5. Why should Marisol read the entire want ads section instead of just the jobs listed under *Office?*

    (1) Employers may list office jobs under many different key words.

    (2) She may decide to change careers.

    (3) She can find out how much employees in other fields are earning.

    (4) The newspaper often lists jobs incorrectly.

6. Write the phrase *Computer exp req* without abbreviations.

    _____

7. Marisol has been limiting her job search to reading the want ads. List three other ways that Marisol could find job leads.

    _____

    _____

8. Marisol receives a telephone call from Louise Graham, who explains that the job advertised in the paper has been filled. But Louise is impressed with Marisol's resume and offers to meet with her to help her find other job leads. To expand her network of contacts, what question should Marisol ask Ms. Graham?

    (1) Do you think I need to go back to school to improve my skills?

    (2) Will you be hiring more office workers in the future?

    (3) Can you suggest other people I could talk to about my career?

    (4) Should I call you back in a few weeks to see if you have any openings?

Feedback

- If you got all of the answers right . . .   you have a good understanding of how to find job leads. You understand the kinds of skills employers look for in a worker. Use the techniques that the video suggests to find job leads in your area of interest.

- If you missed question 1, 2, 3, or 4 . . .   you need to think more about what kinds of skills are important to an employer and how your skills and strengths can help you find a job.

- If you missed question 5 or 6 . . .   you need to learn more about how the want ads can help you find job leads.

- If you missed question 7 or 8 . . .   you need to learn more about other job search strategies that can help you find job ads.

Vocabulary for *Matching Skills and Jobs*

adaptive skills	personality traits or personal qualities
administrator	a person who manages or is in charge of a business
alphabetical	arranged according to the letters of the alphabet
aptitude	ability
categories	groups with similar characteristics
initiative	the ability to use positive energy to begin or complete a task
inventories	tests or evaluations of related skills and abilities
networking	establishing contacts for help and support in the job search
prerequisite skills	skills you must have before you can do a particular job
requirements	skills, training, or conditions that an employer requires
transferable skills	skills that can be used on any job
volunteer work	work or a service that is done by someone who does not receive pay

PBS LiteracyLink®

Now watch Program 2.

After you watch, work on:
- pages 33–46 in this workbook
- Internet activities at www.pbs.org/literacy

AFTER you WATCH

Matching Skills and Jobs

On the following pages, you will learn more about the ideas discussed in the video program and have an opportunity to develop your skills.

Think About the Key Points from the Video Program

To assess your skills, you need to:
- Think about your skills, interests, and experiences.
- Find out about skill **inventories** and tests that may be available to you.
- Think about how your skills can help you achieve your goals for the future.

To find out what kinds of jobs can help you achieve your goals, you need to:
- Think about how your career goals relate to possible jobs.
- Use job postings to find out more about what kind of jobs are available in your community.
- Find work-related contacts through family members, friends, and acquaintances.

Now you are ready to make the job search your job. At this point, you need to:
- Figure out how your skills can meet an employer's needs.
- Use the want ads to find job leads.
- Use all available resources to find job leads.

WORKTIP

As you talk about your career goals with others:
- Be specific about your goals and plans.
- Show interest and excitement when learning more about your career field.
- Don't be a know-it-all. Let the person you are talking to be the expert.
- Ask for information and advice. Then listen and take notes.
- Follow up on every job lead even if the job doesn't seem to be exactly what you were looking for.

Assessing Your Employability

CONSTRUCTION: Gordon is interested in a career in construction, but he isn't sure how to get started. One of his neighbors, Cal Sutton, is a roofer. One evening, Gordon calls first and then pays a visit to Cal. They talk about the roofing business. Impressed with Gordon's **initiative,** Cal tells Gordon that he and his partner are thinking of hiring an assistant. Suddenly, a talk between neighbors has become a job interview. Cal asks Gordon about his skills and strengths. **What skills and strengths do you think Cal might be looking for in an assistant?**

_____

_____

_____

Think about some of your life experiences. In each experience, you mastered new skills or strengthened skills you already had. As a student, you have learned to manage your time, to study and take notes, and to take personal responsibility. All these skills will be valuable to your employer.

Think About the Three Areas of Skills

Adaptive skills are sometimes known as personality traits or personal qualities. These are the skills that make you a good friend, family member, and worker. Adaptive skills include patience, creativity, and cooperation.

You also have **transferable skills.** These are skills, acquired through many life experiences, that you can use on almost any job. You may have a talent for repairing things, making posters and signs, keeping records, or hosting a party. Your transferable skills will help you on any job.

Job-related skills are the skills that you need to fulfill your job duties. If you work in an office, you may need to know how to use a computer or a copier. To be a roofer's assistant, Gordon may need to learn how to lay shingles and patch leaks. Some job-related skills can be learned on the job. Others are **prerequisite skills** you must have before you can be hired.

Assess Your Skills and Strengths

People sometimes think that talking about their skills and strengths is boasting or bragging. But employers want to find out who you are. They need to know what skills you can bring to the workplace. How can you find out more about your skills and strengths so that you can discuss them with employers?

Try an organized approach. First, make a list of your life experiences. Include school, paid work, **volunteer work,** and your experiences in community and religious organizations. For each item on your list, think about the skills you used in that setting.

Second, ask your friends and family for help. Show them your list. They may be able to see skills and strengths you have overlooked.

Third, take tests and inventories. Career counseling services often administer test packages at little or no cost to you. One of the most frequently used tests is the ASVAB (Armed Services Vocational Aptitude Battery). **Aptitude** tests measure your ability to learn new skills and to do well in the career field you have chosen. Other kinds of tests measure specific job skills, such as typing and keyboarding speed.

> **WORKTIP**
>
> As you take tests and inventories:
>
> - Don't be nervous. You cannot fail an aptitude test.
> - Get plenty of rest the night before. You want the test to reflect your best work.
> - Answer questions thoughtfully. Your test results can help you make important career decisions.
> - Always do your best work.

WorkSkills

1. Write *A* if the skill is adaptive and *T* if it is transferable.

    _____ **a.** dependable
    _____ **b.** balancing a checkbook
    _____ **c.** following directions to put something together
    _____ **d.** willing to change
    _____ **e.** reading and taking notes
    _____ **f.** filling out forms
    _____ **g.** hard-working
    _____ **h.** responsible

2. An aptitude test can tell you

    (1) how fast you will someday be able to type
    (2) whether you have the ability to learn the skills you will need in your chosen career
    (3) which adaptive skills you need to do certain jobs
    (4) whether you have all the job-related skills you need to do a particular job

3. What are some skills you can develop during your job search that you can apply once you get a job? List them on a separate piece of paper.

SERVICE: Ramona has been volunteering at her child's school for the last year. She helped to organize a spring fair with game and food booths to help the school raise money. For the event, she had to get city permits and find volunteers to run the booths, do publicity, and sell tickets. She also had to keep records of income and expenses. **What adaptive skills do you think Ramona used to run the spring fair?**

_____

_____

_____

Analyze Your Skills

Employers expect new employees to have the reading, writing, math, and communication skills needed to do the job. If you need to develop these skills, you can get further training.

Employers also look for applicants with specific job-related skills, such as the ability to run a certain machine or to work on an assembly line. Do not be discouraged if you do not have many job-related skills. Your adaptive and transferable skills may help you get a job. These skills come from life experiences. These are skills that employers are willing to pay for.

Read the following list of adaptive skills. Look up any words you don't know. Then put a checkmark by the skills you have. If you have other adaptive skills, add them to the list.

CHECKLIST OF ADAPTIVE SKILLS

☐ adaptable	☐ flexible	☐ motivated
☐ cooperative	☐ friendly	☐ reliable
☐ courteous	☐ honest	☐ responsible
☐ creative	☐ independent	☐ tactful
☐ efficient	☐ positive attitude	☐ understanding
☐ energetic	☐ professional	☐ other: _____

Now do the same thing with this partial list of transferable skills.

CHECKLIST OF TRANSFERABLE SKILLS

☐ communicating with others	☐ repairing equipment
☐ handling cash	☐ speaking a second language
☐ following directions	☐ speaking in public
☐ keeping records	☐ teaching skills to others
☐ organizing materials	☐ troubleshooting
☐ problem solving	☐ writing letters and reports
☐ reading diagrams and maps	☐ other: _____

Next, think about how to market your skills. Analyze each skill. Make sure you know what it means. Think about how that skill could be used on the job you are considering. Then think of one or two examples from your life experience in which you have shown that skill.

For example, suppose Ramona decides to tell an employer that she is a good troubleshooter. A *troubleshooter* is someone who figures out why something isn't working and finds a way to solve the problem. How can Ramona back up her claim? She can use specific experiences in solving problems with the spring fair to demonstrate her troubleshooting abilities.

WorkSkills

1. Check off all the statements that are true.

   _____ **a.** Employers are not interested in your personal qualities.

   _____ **b.** Doing research using the Internet is an example of a transferable skill.

   _____ **c.** Adaptive skills are acquired only in the workplace.

   _____ **d.** Being trustworthy is an adaptive skill.

2. Choose an adaptive skill and a transferable skill from the preceding page. For each, write an example explaining how or when you have used that skill.

   Adaptive Skill: _____

   Example: _____

   Transferable Skill: _____

   Example: _____

WRITE IT

Think about the future. You have the skills you need to get a job, but what skills will you need to advance in your job? Think of a new skill you would like to have. Imagine ways to learn that skill. Then use the following steps to set a goal.

- Define your skill goal. Describe the skill you want to acquire or improve. Be specific. Include how well you expect to be able to do the skill.
- Record a series of steps in your notebook that will lead to your goal.
- For each step, write the date by which you plan to have completed it.
- Record the date when you plan to have finished the steps and acquired your new skill.

Finding Job Leads

SERVICE: Omar wants to be an automotive mechanic, but first he must go back to school for more training. He plans to work part-time while he goes to school. After talking with friends and family, he has three job leads. He could stock shelves at his uncle's grocery store, work as a gasoline station attendant, or be a salesperson at an automotive tire store. Omar would like to find a job that could help him in his career. **Which job do you think would best help Omar gain skills he could use in his career as a mechanic? Explain your thinking.**

_____

_____

_____

WORKTIP

As you look for job leads:

- Talk to everyone you meet about your career goals.
- Communicate the skills you have to offer.
- Represent yourself in a positive light. Employers expect you to talk about your strengths.
- Always put your best foot forward. An employer who can't offer you a job may know someone who can.

Work to Learn New Skills

What can you do to make sure each job you pursue brings you closer to achieving your goals?

Within any career field, there are many different jobs. There are also related careers with jobs that use similar skills to those you will need in your career. Working in a related field can sometimes help you achieve your career goals. With careful planning, you can find jobs that will help you build the skills that you will need in the future. Think of each job as a way to build your skill base, not just a way to make money.

Explore Job Postings

Employers advertise for new workers in many ways. They may run an ad in the newspaper, send job notices out to their current employees, or post the job with a career counseling service. You can find the telephone number for your state's Employment Development Department, or Job Services, in the government pages of your telephone book. Job Services organizes the job postings and makes them available to the public. If you go through their counseling program, they can send you out on interviews for the jobs in which you have an interest.

Study the job posting below.

```
┌────────────────────────────────────────────────────────────────┐
│                     Job Services Office                        │
│    Counselor: Jane R. Kimball      Posting JOB# 1884531-6364   │
│          For the position of: SALESPERSON                      │
│                                                                │
│  Position Description and Requirements: Salesperson—fishing    │
│  equipment. Requires some skills and knowledge in spin, fly,   │
│  and warm-water fishing. Previous sales experience preferred   │
│  but will train the right person. Duties: Selling fishing      │
│  tackle, stocking, cashiering, cleaning.                       │
│                                                                │
│  Work: FULL-TIME    Hours: Arranged   Salary: $6–$7/hr   Days Off: SUNDAY │
└────────────────────────────────────────────────────────────────┘
```

Even before you are ready to start going on job interviews, you can learn about jobs from job postings. Job postings are organized in **categories**. For example, categories may include retail, health care, service, manufacturing, office work, and construction. Within the categories, the postings may be arranged in **alphabetical** order by job title. Read the postings for your career and related fields. Make notes about the duties and **requirements** for each. Think about the range of jobs that can help you reach your career goals.

··

WorkSkills

1. What kinds of information can you gather from the job posting listed above? Check all that apply.

   _____ **a.** the job title for the position that is open
   _____ **b.** the amount of experience required
   _____ **c.** a brief description of the job
   _____ **d.** the name of the employer
   _____ **e.** a list of job duties
   _____ **f.** the employer's phone number
   _____ **g.** the amount you would be paid for the job

2. Think about Omar's situation. How could taking a job pumping gas help him achieve his career goal?

   _____

   _____

   _____

3. Write three reasons to read and study job postings.

   _____

   _____

   _____

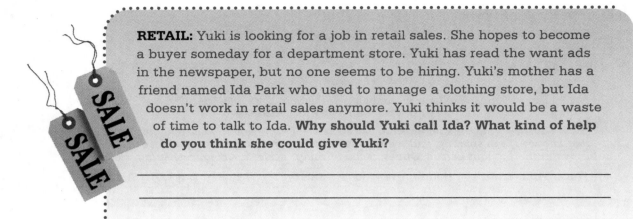

RETAIL: Yuki is looking for a job in retail sales. She hopes to become a buyer someday for a department store. Yuki has read the want ads in the newspaper, but no one seems to be hiring. Yuki's mother has a friend named Ida Park who used to manage a clothing store, but Ida doesn't work in retail sales anymore. Yuki thinks it would be a waste of time to talk to Ida. **Why should Yuki call Ida? What kind of help do you think she could give Yuki?**

_____

_____

_____

You have already seen how information interviews can help you gather information about your career field. You can also use these contacts to get job leads and make new contacts. This process is called **networking.**

Network to Find Leads

In the job search, your contacts form a network. Starting a network is easy. Talk to your friends, family, and neighbors. Ask them to suggest people you can talk to. Then follow through on every suggestion. Each time you talk to a new contact, talk briefly about your career goals. Ask if this contact person can suggest any other people you could interview. Then keep going.

As your network grows, you will learn more about your career field and you will develop job leads. Remember, word-of-mouth is still the most common way in which employers find the workers they need. As you network, you will find out about jobs that will not be advertised anywhere else. Even an employer who has no job openings may know an employer who is hiring.

Organize Your Efforts

As you network, keep a careful record of each interview. Take notes on note cards. Record the following information:
- the name, address, and telephone number of your contact
- your contact's place of business
- any advice or information you gain
- the names and phone numbers of new contacts to make
- any follow-up steps you need to take

One of the keys to networking is to make sure you follow up on leads in a timely way. For each follow-up step you list, set a date for completion and write it on a calendar. Then check your calendar often and do the work.

Keep the Lines of Communication Open

Every contact is important. You never know when you may need to call on someone again for more information. Send a brief letter of thanks after each interview. If you promised to call, send a resume, or follow up in some other way, be sure to follow through on your commitment.

··

WorkSkills

1. A good way to find out about unadvertised job leads is to

    (1) read the newspaper
    (2) network
    (3) read job postings
    (4) keep careful records

2. Which of these questions should you always ask on an interview to expand your network?

    (1) "How much pay should I expect to earn once I am hired?"
    (2) "What skills will I need to succeed in this career?"
    (3) "Do you think I should go back to school for more training?"
    (4) "Are there any other people you suggest that I interview?"

3. Yuki decides to make an appointment to interview Ida. On a separate piece of paper, write a list of five questions and topics that she could discuss with Ida.

COMMUNICATE

When you are on an interview, what should you be doing when the interviewer is talking? You should be listening. Unfortunately, most people use the time when someone else is talking to think about what they are going to say next. Try this exercise to practice your listening skills.

- Ask a friend to read to you from a short magazine or newspaper article for about two minutes. Listen carefully. Then tell the main ideas and as many details as you can back to your friend. How did you do? Did you remember most of the details correctly?
- Now try the same exercise again with a new article. Immediately after your friend stops reading, write down a few notes. Then use your notes to retell the main ideas and details of the article. Did the notes help?
- Practice taking notes as you listen in daily conversation. Write only the most important points.

Making the Job Search Your Job

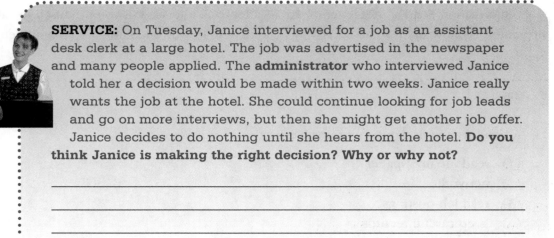

SERVICE: On Tuesday, Janice interviewed for a job as an assistant desk clerk at a large hotel. The job was advertised in the newspaper and many people applied. The **administrator** who interviewed Janice told her a decision would be made within two weeks. Janice really wants the job at the hotel. She could continue looking for job leads and go on more interviews, but then she might get another job offer. Janice decides to do nothing until she hears from the hotel. **Do you think Janice is making the right decision? Why or why not?**

_____

_____

By now, you have a career plan, including career goals and the steps you must take to reach your goals. How can you make your dreams a reality?

Establish a Routine

Start practicing now to be a full-time employee. Get up early, eat a good breakfast, and dress as you would to go to work. Even if you don't have an interview planned, you may have the chance to talk to someone to get information or find a new job lead. Be ready to make a good impression.

Make a list of tasks for the day. Check your calendar. Are there any important follow-up steps that you could complete today? Think about the steps you have written for your career goals. Is there anything you could do today that would help you accomplish one of the next steps in your plan?

Make a schedule for the day. Assign a time to accomplish each task you have on your list. Then follow the schedule. If new opportunities come up, adjust your schedule by moving some tasks to the next day's list.

It may be tempting to sit back and wait for employers to come to you. However, experience shows that successful people and businesses actively seek to achieve their goals.

If you run out of ways to find job leads, you need to broaden your network. Talk again to family and friends. Talk to former employers, former co-workers, friends from school, teachers and counselors from school, and other job seekers. Every time you broaden your network, you increase the number of people who are working to help you find a job.

Search Job Postings

If you are out of job leads and you have time on your hands, pay another visit to the state career counseling service in your area. Remember, job agencies and counseling services post information about the jobs they have available. Job postings are usually grouped by category.

When you find a posting you are interested in, find the job order number and take it to a counselor. If you have the skills required for the job, the counselor can give you the information you need to make an appointment for an interview. You may have to take tests to show you have the skills you need for the job.

WorkSkills

1. Which of the following should you do every day of your job search? Check all that apply.

    _____ **a.** Make a list of tasks for the day.
    _____ **b.** Dress to make a good impression.
    _____ **c.** Schedule at least one information interview.
    _____ **d.** Get an early start.
    _____ **e.** Visit a career counseling service.
    _____ **f.** Review the steps for achieving your career goals.

2. You have talked to your family and friends about your career goals. Whom else could you interview to expand your network?

    _____

    _____

3. After a week goes by, Janice finds out that she didn't get the job at the hotel. She doesn't have any other job interviews lined up. How can she find new job leads? Give three suggestions.

    _____

    _____

    _____

CONSTRUCTION: Daryl wants a career in the construction industry. He worked as a drywall helper for a few months last summer, but he doesn't have any job leads right now. He checked the want ads under Construction, but most of the jobs had titles he had never heard of. Daryl decides to ask his friends for advice on what he should do to find a job. **What advice would you give Daryl? What steps could he take to learn more about his career and find job leads?**

_____

_____

_____

Understand the Organization of the Want Ads

Employers pay to advertise job openings in the classified section of the newspaper. The Employment section of the want ads is organized alphabetically by key words representing job titles, career fields, and sometimes, places of employment. The same kind of job can be listed in more than one place. For example, you may find listings for medical assistant jobs under the key words *Medical Assistant, Health Occupations,* and *Hospital.* It is a good idea to scan all the ads from *A* to *Z.*

Understand Abbreviations

Study the list of abbreviations. Read the two want ads; the first one contains abbreviations, and the second one does not.

appt	appointment	hr	hour	ref	references
asst	assistant	K	thousand	req	required
ben	benefits	max	maximum	sal	salary
comm	commission	min	minimum	sched	schedule
exc, xlnt	excellent	M–F	Monday–Friday	temp	temporary
exp	experience	mo	month	wk	week
DOE	dependent on	nec	necessary	w/	with
	experience	p/t, PT	part-time	wpm	words per minute
f/t, FT	full-time	pref	preferred	yr	year

HOTEL DESK CLERK FT, min 1 yr work exp. req., full ben, sal $14K/yr. Send resume and ref to Orion Hotel, PO Box 1572, Ventura, CA 93008

HOTEL DESK CLERK Full-time, minimum 1 year work experience required, full benefits, salary $14,000 per year. Send resume and references to Orion Hotel, PO Box 1572, Ventura, CA 93008

Answering a Want Ad

Want ads should tell you exactly what to do to apply for the job. Most require you to send a resume. Some direct you to apply in person, and some give you a telephone number to call. Follow the directions in the ad carefully.

Don't be disappointed if you find out an advertised job has already been filled. Instead, use the opportunity to make a new contact. Write down the name of the interviewer and call back in a few days to request an information interview.

The want ads can also help you gather information about your career field. Study the want ads to find out the names of jobs and careers, the starting pay for your target job, and the names of companies that are hiring.

WorkSkills

1. On a separate piece of paper, write this want ad without abbreviations.

DATA ENTRY p/t worker needed now, M-F, 30 hr per wk, some evenings, $8.90/hr to start; keyboarding—40+ wpm req, 1 yr min office exp pref; Call Jeff at (213) 555-5490

2. What kinds of information can you usually learn by reading the want ads? Check all that apply.

_____ **a.** the names of job titles in your career field

_____ **b.** the name of the person who will be your supervisor

_____ **c.** the number of hours you may be asked to work

_____ **d.** the amount of money you can expect as a starting salary

_____ **e.** the job requirements for your target job

_____ **f.** the names of companies that are hiring

_____ **g.** the times at which you can expect a raise or promotion

READ IT

Follow these steps to find key words that relate to your career field.
- Find out which day's paper has the largest classified ad section for your community. Obtain a newspaper for that day.
- Scan the want ads. Each time you find an advertisement related to your career area, write down the key word.
- Tally the number of ads you find under each key word on your list.

Report your findings to your class or a friend.

Review

SERVICE: Kevin wants to work part-time while he takes classes in education at City College. He would like a job working with children, perhaps as a teacher's aide or as a counselor in a day-care facility. Last summer, he was a counselor at a summer camp for children. Kevin speaks Korean and English, plays the piano, and has experience planning arts and crafts activities. He has worked as a volunteer math tutor for 7th graders. In each job, Kevin has shown that he is reliable, hard-working, and patient.

Every day for a week, Kevin has searched the want ads under the key word *children*. He is discouraged because he seldom finds more than one or two jobs listed and they require a college degree or several years of work experience.

1. List three transferable skills that Kevin has gained from previous experiences that he may be able to use in his next job.

   _____

   _____

   _____

2. To find more job leads, why would it be a good idea for Kevin to read the entire want ads section?

   _____

   _____

   _____

   _____

3. Besides reading the want ads, what other strategies could Kevin use to find job leads?

   _____

   _____

   _____

4. Kevin decides to visit a local school and talk to the principal, Kathy Hooper. Kathy tells Kevin that she doesn't have any job openings at her school at the present time. What are some questions that Kevin could ask Kathy to expand his network and find new job leads?

   _____

   _____

   _____

BEFORE you WATCH

program **3**

Applying for Jobs

The video program you are about to watch shows you how to apply for jobs. You will learn how to respond to want ads and other job announcements. You will learn the do's and don'ts of filling out job application forms. The program will also help you see the importance of using your time well and organizing your job search materials carefully.

As you watch, think about which of your life experiences might convince employers that you have the kinds of skills they are looking for. Think about your paid and unpaid work experiences and your school experiences. Also think of people who may be willing to be **references** for you. List them in your notebook or folder.

In the video program, you will learn more about what an employer looks for in an **applicant** and what causes an employer to **screen out** an applicant. Your job application form and **resume** can tell an employer quite a bit about the quality of work you can do. As you watch the video, you will learn tips for filling out forms and talking to employers directly. These tips can help you always put your best foot forward.

OBJECTIVES

In this lesson, you will work with the following concepts and skills:

1. Exploring the application process
2. Understanding how employers screen job seekers
3. Completing job application forms

Sneak Preview

This exercise previews some of the concepts from Program 3. After you answer the questions, use the Feedback on page 49 to help set your learning goals.

MANUFACTURING: Neal is applying for a job in a print shop. His main job duty would be using the different copiers in the shop to fill printing orders from customers. He might also be asked to help customers at the counter, record their orders on Job Order forms, and accept payments from customers.

Neal visited the printing shop and talked to the owner, Naomi Kang. She asked him to fill out an application form. Here is Neal's completed work history section of the application.

Work History: List all jobs that you have had in the past ten years or since attending school as a full-time student. List your most recent job first. You may include volunteer work.

EMPLOYER	Zesto's Pizza	YOUR JOB TITLE	Counter worker
ADDRESS	1025 N. Main Street	WORK PERFORMED	Took orders, gave orders to cook, collected money, made change, helped to open and close the restaurant.
CITY/STATE/ZIP	Radcliff, KY 40160		
SUPERVISOR	Steve Prow PHONE #		
DATES EMPLOYED (MO/YR)			
FROM 1997 TO last month		REASON FOR LEAVING	I need a job that pays more money.
PAY $5.50 per hour			
EMPLOYER	Toy Village	YOUR JOB TITLE	Bicycle Assembler
ADDRESS	205 E. Broadway Avenue	WORK PERFORMED	Assembled bikes for customers, helped customers load the bikes in their cars.
CITY/STATE/ZIP	Radcliff, KY 40160		
SUPERVISOR	Lynn Logan PHONE # (502)555-1047		
DATES EMPLOYED (MO/YR)			
FROM December 1996 TO March 1997		REASON FOR LEAVING	The job was only part-time and I needed to work more hours.
PAY $5.35 per hour plus tips			

Answer these questions based on the situation described on page 48.

1. Why would it be important to Naomi Kang to ensure that Neal answered every question truthfully?

   _____

   _____

2. **a.** Neal left one item blank on the application. Which one?

   _____

   b. Why is it important for Neal to fill in the application completely?

   _____

3. Based on the completed form, which of the following is a true statement?

   (1) Naomi cannot tell how many months Neal worked at Zesto's Pizza.
   (2) Neal worked at least one year at Toy Village.
   (3) Both Neal's work experiences were full-time jobs.
   (4) Neal earned at least $500 per month at Toy Village.

Feedback

- If you got all of the answers right . . .

  you have a foundation for using the application process to your advantage. Concentrate on the suggestions in the video that will help you make a good impression.

- If you missed question 1 . . .

  you need to think more about how the information on an application form is used to screen potential employees.

- If you missed question 2 or 3 . . .

  you need to practice filling out job application forms neatly and completely.

Vocabulary for *Applying for Jobs*

annual wage	the amount of pay an employee earns in one year
applicant	someone who applies for a job
background checks	examinations of the facts about an applicant's education and work experiences
candidate	a person who is seeking a job
not applicable	abbreviated N/A, a phrase used on a form to show that an item does not apply to the person who filled it out
open-ended questions	questions that do not have one right answer
personnel office	a workplace department that handles hiring and benefits. Often called *human resources department.*
portfolio	a collection of a person's best work
reasonable accommodations	arrangements or equipment needed to enable a special-needs individual to do a job, such as a large-type computer keyboard for the sight-impaired
references	people who know an applicant well and can talk about his or her work habits and skills
requirements	skills and experiences needed to do a certain job
resume	a short summary of a job applicant's skills and experiences
screen out	to reject a job applicant before the interview stage
temporary job	a job that lasts for a limited time

PBS
LiteracyLink®

Now watch Program 3.

After you watch, work on:
- pages 51–64 in this workbook
- Internet activities at www.pbs.org/literacy

AFTER YOU WATCH

program 3

Applying for Jobs

On the following pages, you will learn more about the ideas discussed in the video program and have an opportunity to develop your skills.

Think About the Key Points from the Video Program

To apply for a job, you need to:
- Find out exactly what an employer wants when you apply for a specific job.
- Know how to make a good impression over the telephone and in person.
- Be prepared to fill out a job application form neatly and completely.

To make a good impression, you need to:
- Understand how employers screen job seekers.
- Think about what personal references to use.
- Learn how to focus on your positive achievements.

When you apply for a job, you will be asked to fill out a job application form. To improve your chances of getting the job, you need to:
- Understand the purpose of job application forms.
- Gather the information you will need to complete the form.
- Know how to check your form so that it makes the best impression.

Figuring Out the Application Process

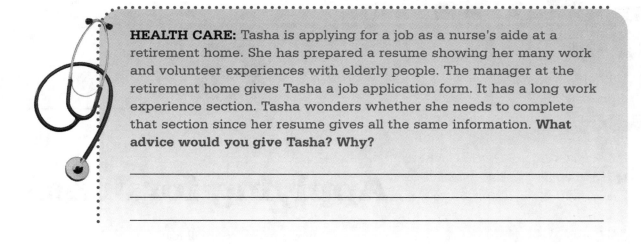

HEALTH CARE: Tasha is applying for a job as a nurse's aide at a retirement home. She has prepared a resume showing her many work and volunteer experiences with elderly people. The manager at the retirement home gives Tasha a job application form. It has a long work experience section. Tasha wonders whether she needs to complete that section since her resume gives all the same information. **What advice would you give Tasha? Why?**

_____

_____

_____

To find the right person for a job, employers need information. They need to learn about the experience, skills, work habits, attitudes, and interests of each **applicant.** This helps employers to make good decisions.

Get Specific Instructions

Employers tailor the job application process to fit the job opening. Most applicants are required to fill out a job application form. But other **requirements** may differ. For many jobs, you will be asked to submit a resume. In artistic fields, you may be asked to prepare a **portfolio** showing samples of your work. You may be interviewed by the owner of the business, a committee of workers, a supervisor, or a worker from the **personnel office**.

When you apply for a job, you need to find out exactly what process the employer will use to screen the applicants for the job. If you are answering a want ad, follow the directions in the ad carefully. If you hear about a job opening, call the employer on the telephone and ask for instructions. Then follow the instructions to the best of your ability.

Do Your Best Work

Job application forms and resumes are both samples of the quality of work that you can do. They contain some of the same information, but they are organized differently.

On your resume, you decide what information to include and how to express it. In contrast, the job application form has been designed by the employer. Since every applicant must fill out the same form, the employer can easily compare the skills and experience of the applicants.

Fill in every space on a job application form. Print your answers neatly. Try to avoid scratching out answers, smudging the paper, or folding the form.

Make a Good Impression

Employers may make the final hiring decisions, but other people in the workplace often influence their decisions. Imagine you are visiting a business to drop off your job application form. As you enter the building and walk down the hall to the personnel office, you may encounter receptionists, security guards, file clerks, secretaries, and many other workers who help the business run smoothly. Each of these contacts is an opportunity to make a good impression.

WORKTIP

When you apply for a job:

- Make every contact with the employer a positive experience.
- Dress to make a good impression, even if you are only stopping by to pick up or drop off an application. Wear conservative clothes that are clean and neat.
- Carefully check your application for errors.
- If your application looks messy, pick up another form and re-copy it.

WorkSkills

1. Which of the following is a true statement?

    (1) If you have a resume, you will not have to fill out job application forms.
    (2) Each question on the job application form is important.
    (3) Employers won't care if you leave some application questions blank.
    (4) Employers use the same application process for every job opening.

2. Suppose you hear about a job opening from a friend. What should you do to apply for the job?

    (1) Drop off a copy of your resume at the personnel office.
    (2) Call the employer's office and ask the person who answers the phone to mail you a job application form.
    (3) Visit the office and request an interview for the job.
    (4) Call the employer and ask how to apply; then follow the directions exactly.

3. After work, Tasha works out at a gym near the retirement home. She decides to drop off her completed job application form after she works out on Wednesday. How should Tasha be dressed when she drops off the application form? Why?

    _____

    _____

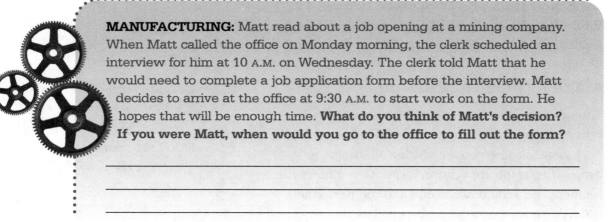

MANUFACTURING: Matt read about a job opening at a mining company. When Matt called the office on Monday morning, the clerk scheduled an interview for him at 10 A.M. on Wednesday. The clerk told Matt that he would need to complete a job application form before the interview. Matt decides to arrive at the office at 9:30 A.M. to start work on the form. He hopes that will be enough time. **What do you think of Matt's decision? If you were Matt, when would you go to the office to fill out the form?**

_____

_____

_____

Completing a job application form is an important step toward getting hired. Make sure you give it the effort it deserves.

Avoid Common Mistakes on Applications

Filling out an application form is not hard, but it can be stressful and frustrating. These hints and tips can help you avoid the common mistakes many job applicants make.

- **Whenever possible, pick up the application form the day before your interview.** Then fill the application out at home. If a form looks difficult, photocopy it before you begin. Then practice writing your responses on the photocopy before completing the actual form.

- **Read the form before you write anything.** Pay close attention to the directions. When you are ready to write, use a pen. Black ink is often required. Buy erasable pens so that you can change answers easily.

- **You must write something in every space for your application to be complete.** If a question does not apply to you, draw a short line in the blank like this: ——. Or write N/A, which means **not applicable**.

- **Your application will not be considered unless it is signed and dated.** By signing the application, you are agreeing that the information you have given on the form is true. Always tell the truth. If an employer finds out that your application contains false information, you will not be hired.

- **Finally, check your application for mistakes before you turn it in.** Check telephone numbers carefully, especially your own. Check your spelling. Remember that the application form shows the quality of work that you can do. If you make careless mistakes, you may not be considered for the job.

Some application questions require you to write several sentences or a paragraph. Employers include these questions to see how well you write. Before you fill out this portion of an application form, draft your answer in your notebook or folder. Revise and edit, keeping these tips in mind:

- Always answer these types of questions in complete sentences.
- Check your spelling carefully.
- Make sure to stay on topic and completely answer the question asked.
- Copy the final draft onto the application form.

WorkSkills

1. Which of these tips can help you do your best to fill out a job application form? Check all that apply.

    _____ a. If the form looks difficult, use a pencil with a good eraser.
    _____ b. Make sure you sign and date your application.
    _____ c. Write something in every blank space.
    _____ d. Write N/A next to questions you do not want to answer.
    _____ e. Read the entire form before you write anything.

2. Matt's application form has many small spaces. He is concerned about filling it out neatly. What could he do?

    _____

3. One question on Matt's application form reads, "Why do you want to work for AA Mining?" Matt writes the following: *Been interested in mining and construction equipment all my life. Want to someday become an operating engineer. I would also like to help build houses.* **Matt could improve his job chances if his answer were better written. Rewrite his answer below.**

    _____
    _____
    _____

WRITE IT

When applying for a job, you need to know the facts about your education, work history, and volunteer experiences. Take time now to create a fact sheet, making sure all information is accurate and spelled correctly.

- Make a list of your work, education, and volunteer experiences.
- List the starting and ending dates for each experience.
- For each activity, write the name of someone you could use as a reference.
- Summarize the duties or activities for each experience.

Recopy the information onto the Information Worksheet on page 179.

Learning How Employers Screen Job Seekers

SERVICE: Joya worked as a service dispatcher for a plumbing business for six months. When she heard rumors that the company was going to close, she started looking for other work. She took a **temporary job** in an office for two months. Now Joya is looking for work again. She wants to find the best way to explain her work history to employers. She knows employers might frown on her leaving the dispatcher job after only six months. **If you were Joya, what would you write in the space on the job application form that asks your reasons for leaving the job at the plumbing business?**

_____

_____

A hiring mistake can be costly for employers, so they use several strategies to screen applicants and make sure they are hiring the best **candidate** for the job.

Think About How Employers Use Job Application Forms

Employers use job application forms to screen job applicants. Employers may reject an applicant for the following reasons:

Lack of Skills: Each job requires a certain set of skills. Employers may be willing to train you to do some of those skills, but probably not all of them. If you lack basic skills for the job, the employer may not hire you.

Not Following Directions: An employer assumes you have done your best work to fill out your job application form correctly. If you have ignored the directions, the employer may be concerned that you cannot follow directions carefully.

Messy Writing: If an employer cannot read what you have written, your application may be rejected.

Think About How Employers Use Resumes

A resume is a summary of your skills and experience. At a glance, an employer can see whether you have the background and skills to do the job. Your resume also shows an employer how well you write and organize information. If you submit a resume with errors, an employer may question your ability to read carefully and pay attention to details.

Think About How Employers Use Information from Other Sources

If your application or resume interests an employer, the employer will give you an interview. Interviews help the employer get to know you better and see how well you communicate.

You may also be given tests to measure your work skills. Do the best you can. You don't need to have the best score of all the applicants; you just need to meet the requirements of the job.

Most employers conduct **background checks** to make sure the information that you have stated in your application form and resume is true. Employers will call your personal references for more information about your skills, attitude, and work habits. They may call previous employers to verify the dates you were employed. For some jobs, employers require drug tests and more thorough background checks.

WORKTIP

As you select personal references:

- Choose people who know something about your work habits. A supervisor or a teacher is a better choice than your best friend.
- Ask people's permission to list them as references.
- See Preparing a List of References on page 184.

WorkSkills

1. A data entry job requires the ability to pay close attention to details. Which of these is the most likely to cause an employer to reject an applicant for a data entry job?

    (1) completing a job application form using blue ink
    (2) writing N/A in two of the blanks
    (3) submitting an application form with many errors
    (4) having a signature that is hard to read

2. Why is it important to follow directions on job application forms exactly? Write your answer on a separate piece of paper.

3. Gary had a job as a parking attendant for 3 months. Then he was out of work for 6 months before going back to school. Rather than explain to an employer why he was out of work for so long, he decides to claim that the parking attendant job lasted for 9 months. Do you think Gary's plan is a good one? Explain your thinking. Write your answer on a separate piece of paper.

SERVICE: Monica is interviewing for a clerk-typist job with the local school district. Her main job duty would be filing student records. Monica is an excellent typist, but she hasn't had any filing experience. She did volunteer one summer at the public library where she had the job of reshelving books. Her interviewer asks, "What experiences have you had that will help you succeed in this job?" **How can Monica use her experience at the library to show that she has an aptitude for filing?**

_____

_____

Compare Your Skills with the Job Requirements

To find the best employee for the job, an employer compares each applicant's skills with the job requirements. Emphasize your ability to learn on the job. Few workers are ready to perform all the duties of a new job. Every employee needs some training. If you have a good attitude and the ability to learn, you may be hired.

To convince an employer to give you a chance, you need to know your strengths and weaknesses. Always emphasize your strong points. If you are asked about a weak area, talk about what you have done to overcome it.

Be Positive

In every interaction with a potential employer, be sure to give information that makes you a candidate for the job. Never volunteer information that may cause the employer to screen you out.

Employers often ask **open-ended questions** to find out more about an applicant's attitudes toward work. A common question is "Tell me about yourself." Think about how you would answer this question. Think about what information an employer would be interested in.

Open-ended questions are opportunities to talk about your strengths and job-related skills. Do not talk about your family or personal life. Instead, use the opportunity to convince the interviewer that you will bring a positive attitude and good work skills to the workplace.

Emphasize Your Adaptive Skills

As employers read your job application and resume, they are reading between the lines to discover your work habits and skills. As you answer their interview questions, they are listening to discover your work attitudes.

You can show employers that you have the right attitude by being positive about your life experiences. Even experiences that didn't turn out the way you wanted can be positive if you can show that you have learned from them.

WorkSkills

Write *True* if the statement is true; *False* if it is false.

_____ 1. If you don't meet every job requirement, you cannot be hired for a job.

_____ 2. Employers are interested in your attitudes about work.

_____ 3. If you were late to work often on your last job, you should mention this at the beginning of your job interview.

_____ 4. If you are asked directly about a weak area, you should explain why the weakness is not your fault.

5. A typical question on a job application is "What are your strengths?" Answer this question in three sentences.

_____

_____

_____

6. Monica is asked the open-ended question "Why should we hire you?" What should she emphasize in her answer?

_____

WRITE IT

When submitting an application, you may want to include a cover letter. To do so, write three paragraphs, as follows:

- Paragraph 1: Explain why you are writing. Tell what job you are applying for and how you found out about the job.
- Paragraph 2: Describe your skills and strengths.
- Paragraph 3: Ask for an interview. Thank the employer for considering your request.

On a separate piece of paper, write a cover letter. Have someone else read your letter. Consider any suggestions; then revise your letter. **Refer to the How to Type a Business Letter and Sample Cover Letter on pages 182 and 183 in the Reference Handbook.**

Completing Job Application Forms

RETAIL: Ky hears about a job opening at Carpet Castle from his neighbor. His neighbor tells him that the employer, Daryl Sealove, is looking for someone who does neat and careful work and is good at following directions. Daryl also wants an employee who has a friendly manner and good communication skills. **What can Ky do during the job application process to show Daryl that he has these skills?**

_____

_____

WORKTIP

Before you turn in your job application form:

- Read it once from start to finish.
- Erase any smudges or stray marks.
- Make sure you have written something in every space.
- Make sure you have signed and dated the application.

In a way, filling out a job application is a kind of test. The employer is testing your ability to follow directions, do neat and accurate work, and solve problems. Do your best work. The following suggestions will help:

- Plan what you are going to write before you begin.
- Carefully fill out the application form from start to finish. Too many people become careless by the end.
- If you have not had many jobs in the past, list other kinds of work experience, including part-time work and volunteer work.
- If you must fill out an application at the interview, bring a completed Information Worksheet with you and copy the information onto the employer's form. (See page 179 in the Reference Handbook.)

MATH MATTERS

Some work history sections require you to state your earnings as a monthly or **annual wage**. To estimate how much you made in one year and per month, begin by multiplying your hourly wage by the number of hours you worked per week. Then multiply by 52 (weeks) to find the total annual, or yearly, wage. Divide the annual amount by 12 (months) to find the monthly wage.

Find the annual and monthly wages for a job that pays $7 per hour for 40 hours of work per week.

WorkSkills

Think of a job that you would like to have. Apply for it by completing the form on pages 61–63. Write the job title here and keep it in mind as you fill out the application.

National Industries, Inc.　　　　　　　　　**Application for Employment**

General Information

Name _____　Today's Date _____
　　　　LAST　　　　　　FIRST　　　　　MIDDLE

Address _____
　　　　NO.　STREET　　　　　　　　　CITY　　　　　STATE　　ZIP CODE

Do you have any legal right to work and be employed in the U.S.?　　Yes ☐　　No ☐
Proof of identity and legal authority to work in the U.S. is a condition of employment.

Person to be notified in case of accident or emergency?

_____
NAME　　　　　　　　　　　　　　PHONE

_____
ADDRESS

Have you ever been convicted of a crime (excluding traffic violations)?　　Yes ☐　　No ☐
If yes, describe in full.

_____

_____

Position applied for _____　Rate of pay expected $ _____ per _____

On what date will you be available for work? _____

Education

High School Name _____

City/State _____　Highest Grade Completed _____

Universities, Colleges, Trade Schools, Other	City/State	Dates (Mo. & Yr.) From　To	Course of Study	License, Certificate, Degree

List any special knowledge or skills gained through hobbies or independent study that relate to the job for which you are applying.

_____

_____

Skills

Typing Speed _____　Shorthand Speed _____　Fast Notes Speed _____

Office Equipment Operated _____

Type of Computers Used _____

Other Work Skills _____

Military Service

Were you in the U.S. Armed Forces?   Yes ❑   No ❑   If yes, what branch? _____

List duties in the service, including special training, that relate to the job for which you are applying. _____

_____

_____

Work Experience

Please list the last three jobs you have had. You may include part-time jobs, self-employment, and volunteer or community service work. Start with your most recent job.

NAME OF EMPLOYER	YOUR JOB TITLE
ADDRESS	DESCRIBE YOUR JOB DUTIES
CITY/ STATE	
SUPERVISOR'S NAME & TELEPHONE	
DATE STARTED / DATE ENDED / PAY	REASON FOR LEAVING

NAME OF EMPLOYER	YOUR JOB TITLE
ADDRESS	DESCRIBE YOUR JOB DUTIES
CITY/STATE	
SUPERVISOR'S NAME & TELEPHONE	
DATE STARTED / DATE ENDED / PAY	REASON FOR LEAVING

NAME OF EMPLOYER	YOUR JOB TITLE
ADDRESS	DESCRIBE YOUR JOB DUTIES
CITY/STATE	
SUPERVISOR'S NAME & TELEPHONE	
DATE STARTED / DATE ENDED / PAY	REASON FOR LEAVING

Personal References
List three references. Do not include relatives or employees of this company.

Full Name	Address	Phone	Relationship

Unemployed Periods

If there are any unemployed periods of a month or more not accounted for in your application, please explain them here. Provide beginning and ending dates and reason.

FROM   TO   REASON

FROM   TO   REASON

Health Information

Are you able to perform the duties of the position for which you are applying with **reasonable accommodations?** Yes ❑   No ❑

If necessary, please describe what types of reasonable accommodations are needed.

Career Goals

Why are you interested in working for National Industries, and what are your career goals?

Reference Checks and Signature

May we contact your present or last employer about you? Yes ❑   No ❑

If not, why not?

Please read the following and then sign your name below.

In consideration of my employment, I agree to conform to the rules and standards of National Industries. I declare my answers to the questions on this application are true. I agree that any false statement or misrepresentation on this application will be cause for refusal to hire or immediate dismissal. I also understand that all offers of employment are conditioned on the provision of satisfactory proof of my identity and legal authority to work in the United States.

SIGNATURE   DATE

Review

SERVICE: Sharon read the want ads and saw a job for a travel clerk. Her main job duty would be helping customers make travel plans. She would answer telephones, greet customers, provide information, and refer customers to ticket agents.

Sharon called the telephone number in the ad to find out more about the application process. She spoke directly to the manager, Ed Bowen. He gave her an appointment for an interview and asked her to bring a resume. He told her that she would also be required to complete a job application form.

Sharon picked up the application form the day before the interview. The form was long with many small spaces. Sharon filled it out as neatly as she could. Part of her completed form is shown below.

EDUCATION: Name and Location of School (City, State)	Dates		Subjects Studied
	TO:	FROM:	
Orem High School, Orem, UT	9/93	5/97	Speech, Bookkeeping

List any special skills you have that may relate to the job for which you have applied.

I enjoy art and can hand letter posters. I also have experience making flyers using the computer. I am friendly and enjoy meeting the public.

1. Why would the employer ask Sharon for both a resume and a job application form?

   _____

   _____

2. List three mistakes Sharon could make on her job application form that might cause an employer to reject her application.

   _____

   _____

   _____

3. Even though Sharon's special skills are not required for the job, what could she say about them that would help her to get the job?

   _____

   _____

   _____

BEFORE you WATCH

WATCH

Resumes, Tests, and Choices

The video program you are about to watch shows how resumes fit into the application process. It will show you what makes a good resume. It will also explain more about how employers use tests and background checks to screen applicants.

As you continue your job search, you will need to think about your personal needs. The video program will help you **evaluate** important **factors** that can affect whether a job is right for you.

Once you begin interviewing, you may receive one or more job offers. You will need to compare jobs and employers to choose the best job for you. The video program will help you compare salary, benefits, and hours. It will also show you how to learn more about a company before you accept a job.

Sneak Preview

This exercise previews some of the concepts from Program 4. After you answer the questions, use the Feedback on page 67 to help set your learning goals.

MANUFACTURING: Marko is interested in designing and building furniture. He hopes someday to have his own company and build his own designs. Marko learned about a job opening at a sofa factory from one of his neighbors. His job would be to rebuild used sofas and chairs by removing the old covers and padding, fixing sections of the frames, and then using new materials to pad and cover the furniture. Marko thinks the job would help him gain more skills in working with furniture.

To apply for the job, Marko needs to submit a resume. A portion of his resume is shown below.

Skills Summary	Highly motivated, energetic worker with excellent woodworking skills who is eager to learn about all aspects of building furniture.
Work Experience	• **Metro Fencing,** Fence Installation Helper, 7/96 to Present *Duties: Trying to help fence installers put in wood and chain-link fences. Transporting tools and materials to and from the work site.* • **City Recreation,** Center Volunteer, 4/94 to 2/98 *Duties: Donated my time to repair furniture, build cabinets, and help paint a mural in my spare time to improve the local community center in my neighborhood.*
Education	Graduated from South High School, Reno, NV in 1994 Work-related Courses: Metal Shop, Art and Design, and Carpentry.

Answer these questions based on the situation described above.

1. Marko claims to have excellent woodworking skills. What experiences does he have to back up this claim?

_____

_____

_____

2. How could Marko improve the section explaining his job duties at Metro Fencing?

_____

_____

3. According to the situation, what factor is most important to Marko in deciding which jobs to pursue?

   (1) working around his school schedule
   (2) receiving good health benefits
   (3) learning skills to help his career
   (4) earning at least $20,000 per year

4. Before Marko goes on his interview at the sofa factory, he wants to find out how long the company has been in business. Name three sources Marko could use to find this information.

_____

_____

Feedback

- If you got all of the answers right . . .   you have a foundation for writing your resume and evaluating job opportunities. As you pursue job leads, think about what kinds of jobs can meet your career goals and personal needs.

- If you missed question 1 . . .   you need to learn more about the purpose of a resume and how it is used by employers to screen job seekers.

- If you missed question 2 . . .   you need to learn more about how to avoid common mistakes in writing resumes.

- If you missed question 3 . . .   you need to think about how your personal needs can affect your career decisions.

- If you missed question 4 . . .   you need to learn how to research information about a potential employer.

....

Answers for Sneak Preview:

1. He repaired furniture and built cabinets at the recreation center. He also took a carpentry class in high school. 2. He needs to use stronger action verbs, avoiding use of words such as *trying*. 3. Choice (3) 4. Any of the following: the public library, the Internet, the chamber of commerce, the sofa factory

Vocabulary for *Managing Your Job Search*

action verb	a word that plainly tells what someone does, for instance, *build, drive,* and *write*
commitment	a pledge or promise to do something
commuting	traveling to and from work
cons	reasons *not* to take a job
discriminate	to make a hiring decision based on some characteristic other than a person's ability to do the job
documents	written or printed papers that contain information
evaluate	to decide the worth of something
factors	working conditions and facts about a job that influence a job seeker's evaluation of a job
overtime pay	wages paid when an employee works extra hours
proofread	to carefully read a message to find and correct errors
pros	reasons to take a job
recommendation	a statement about a worker's skills and attitude
skills summary	on a resume, a brief statement summarizing a person's skills and goals
verify	to make sure information is true
work environment	the surroundings and conditions in which employees do their job

Now watch Program 4.

After you watch, work on:
- pages 69–82 in this workbook
- Internet activities at www.pbs.org/literacy

PBS **LiteracyLink®**

AFTER·you·WATCH

Resumes, Tests, and Choices

WORKTIP

As you prepare to talk to employers about job openings:

- Think about how your work experiences demonstrate that you are dependable and trustworthy.
- Think about how your educational accomplishments show that you are a hard worker and a problem solver.
- Think about how your hobbies and other interests show that you are creative and motivated.

On the following pages, you will learn more about the ideas discussed in the video program and have an opportunity to develop your skills.

Think About the Key Points from the Video Program

To write a resume, you need to:
- Understand the purpose of a resume.
- Describe how your skills and accomplishments match those related to the job you are applying for.
- Learn how to make your resume readable and free of errors.

As you think about what jobs to apply for, you need to:
- Think about your personal needs.
- Learn how to evaluate job opportunities.
- Think about what you have to gain from a particular job and whether you can make a **commitment** to stay on the job.

As you consider job offers, you need to:
- Think about the **pros** and **cons** of each job.
- Think about what you have to gain from each job opportunity.
- Find out more about the companies where you are considering going to work.

Understanding the Purposes of Resumes

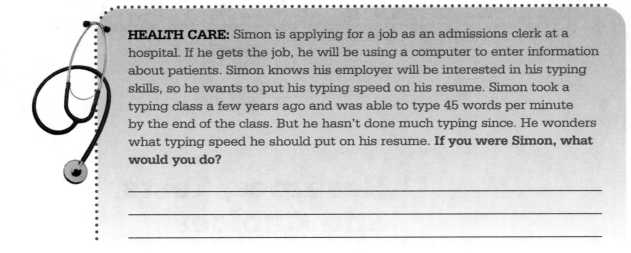

HEALTH CARE: Simon is applying for a job as an admissions clerk at a hospital. If he gets the job, he will be using a computer to enter information about patients. Simon knows his employer will be interested in his typing skills, so he wants to put his typing speed on his resume. Simon took a typing class a few years ago and was able to type 45 words per minute by the end of the class. But he hasn't done much typing since. He wonders what typing speed he should put on his resume. **If you were Simon, what would you do?**

_____

_____

_____

A resume introduces you and your skills to an employer. Like a job application form, a resume includes facts about your work history, education, and volunteer work. But unlike the job application form, your resume is designed and written by you.

Learn How Employers Use Resumes

Resumes are a way for employers to screen the applicants for a job. At a glance, an employer can see whether an applicant has the necessary skills, training, and experience to go on to the next step in the application process—the interview.

Your resume is also a sample of your work. To make a good impression, your resume should be well organized, neat, and easy to read. If you are applying for a job in which you are required to write letters and other business **documents,** you should take extra care to make sure your resume is error-free.

Not all jobs require a resume. Some entry-level positions require applicants to complete only a job application form. If you are not sure whether a resume is required for a specific job, call the employer and ask about the application process.

Learn How Employers Test Applicants and Check Facts

In your resume, you claim to have certain skills, work experience, and training. If employers are interested in hiring you, they may require you to take skills tests to check the facts on your resume and learn more about your abilities. They also may ask you to take tests measuring your knowledge of safety and work practices.

Many employers use drug tests to screen applicants for drug use. Employees who use drugs are less productive and may place themselves and other workers in danger. Employers probably will not hire an applicant who tests positive for drug use.

Most employers do a background check. Your potential employer will call your references and previous supervisors to **verify,** or check, the facts on your resume. Some employers may take your fingerprints for further background checks.

Make sure the information on your resume is true. If an employer discovers that you lied about one thing, he or she may assume other information is false as well. The employer probably will not hire you.

WORKTIP

To find out more about skills tests:

- Call the employer and ask which skills tests are part of the application process.
- Make an appointment with a counselor at a career counseling service where you can take practice skills tests.
- Ask an instructor or a vocational counselor at your school for help.

WorkSkills

1. Explain how a resume differs from a job application form.

   _____

   _____

2. Why is it important to include only true information in the section of your resume explaining your work experience?

   _____

   _____

3. Check all the statements that are true.

   _____ **a.** Even the best resumes usually have some typing errors.
   _____ **b.** You must submit a resume for each job you apply for.
   _____ **c.** A resume gives information about your skills, education, and work experience.
   _____ **d.** If your resume is poorly organized and full of errors, the employer may not consider you for the job.

RETAIL: Huong would like to find a sales job in a clothing store. She makes many of her own clothes and understands how to spot high-quality fabrics. She reads fashion magazines and follows the latest styles and trends. Huong also enjoys helping her friends shop for clothes for special occasions. Huong wants to start her resume with **a skills summary,** a brief statement about her skills and goals. **Use the information about Huong to write a skills summary for her resume.**

_____

_____

Write Your Resume

A resume is a summary of information about you. To make the information easy to read, organize it into sections. Common headings are _Skills Summary, Work Experience, Education,_ and _References_.

Education refers to high school, college, and vocational school experiences. List the school name and location, any degrees or credits earned, the area of study, and the year that you completed the program.

Work Experience includes full- and part-time jobs and volunteer work. For each experience, write the period of time you worked (use months and years), your title or position, and the name and location of the company. Then write a brief description of your job duties. Begin each phrase in the description with a strong **action verb.**

In each section, start with your most recent experience, then work back in time. **Study the sample resumes on pages 180 and 181 in the Reference Handbook.**

Resume Tips

Follow these tips to make a good impression with your resume:
- **Do not include personal information.** Include only your name, address, and daytime phone numbers. You may also include e-mail or fax addresses. Never include your age, nationality, height, or weight. These facts could be used to **discriminate** against you.
- **Keep it short**. A resume is a one-page outline of your skills and experiences. Write using short, clear phrases.
- **Use strong action verbs**. Choose words that sound confident and positive. Examples include _organized, created, built, managed, assisted, established, installed, wrote, drove, cleaned, assembled._ Avoid meaningless words such as _considered, tried to,_ and _meant to._

Prepare the Final Product

To make the best possible impression, use a computer and high-quality printer to produce the final copy of your resume. If you do not have access to a computer, you may want to pay a resume service to produce the final copy. In either case, be sure to have a career counselor, instructor, or another qualified person **proofread** your resume. Then go to a copy center and copy it onto high-quality, nonerasable bond paper.

WorkSkills

1. Why is it a bad idea to include information about your personal appearance on your resume?

   _____

   _____

2. Which of these phrases begins with a strong action verb?

   (1) Realized our sales needed to improve
   (2) Considered ways to increase sales
   (3) Developed a plan to double our sales
   (4) Tried to think of ways to solve our problem with low sales

3. Read the following information from the Work Experience section of Huong's resume:

E X P E R I E N C E	
1994–1996	**Fabric World**, Santa Monica, CA
	Duties: Helped customers find patterns and notions, operated cash register, collected money, and made change.

   The *Work Experience* section can also include volunteer or unpaid work. List two things you know about Huong that she could add to her entry.

   _____

   _____

READ IT

The want ads often contain meaningful phrases that you can use to describe your skills and strengths. Read through the advertisements in the classified section of a newspaper. If your local newspaper does not have many ads, go to a newsstand and buy a copy of a newspaper from a major city. **As you read the ads, make a list in your notebook or on a separate piece of paper of at least ten descriptive words or phrases that could apply to you.**

Deciding Which Job Openings to Pursue

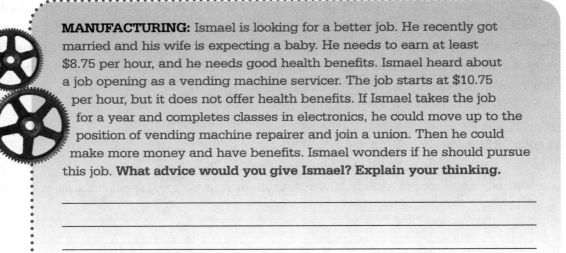

MANUFACTURING: Ismael is looking for a better job. He recently got married and his wife is expecting a baby. He needs to earn at least $8.75 per hour, and he needs good health benefits. Ismael heard about a job opening as a vending machine servicer. The job starts at $10.75 per hour, but it does not offer health benefits. If Ismael takes the job for a year and completes classes in electronics, he could move up to the position of vending machine repairer and join a union. Then he could make more money and have benefits. Ismael wonders if he should pursue this job. **What advice would you give Ismael? Explain your thinking.**

_____

_____

As you read the want ads and search job postings, you may find dozens of jobs for which you could apply. But all job opportunities are not equal. Before you apply for a job, you need to evaluate whether that job will meet your personal needs and career goals.

Think About Your Needs

Different factors are important in analyzing whether a job opening could be right for you. Whether you should apply for a job depends on your priorities. For example, is it more important for you to earn a high wage or to work close to home? Are health benefits a must or would you give up benefits to have a more flexible work schedule?

Think about these factors:
- How much money do you need to earn?
- Would you rather have an hourly wage or earn a monthly salary?
- Do you need health benefits?
- Do you need life insurance and a retirement plan?
- Are **commuting** distance and time important to you?
- Do you need a certain work schedule or can you be flexible?
- Do you plan to go back to school for more training or do you need to find a company that offers on-the-job training?
- Do you need a job that will help you advance within your career field?
- Are there personal needs that must be considered, such as child care, transportation, or your school schedule?

Set Priorities

Deciding what factors are important to you can help you narrow your job search. You may not be able to find a job that will satisfy every one of your personal requirements. But setting priorities can help you focus on the most important factors to look for in a job.

To set priorities, make a list of the factors that are important to you in choosing a job. Use the questions on page 74 to help you make a list. Then number the list according to your priorities. Put *1* by the most important factor, *2* by the second most important factor, and so on. You can use this list to decide if a job meets your needs.

> ### WORKTIP
>
> As you find out more about job openings:
> - Think about your part in the screening process. While the employer is deciding if you are the right person for the job, you are deciding if the job is right for you.
> - Don't accept a job that doesn't meet your important needs unless you can find another way to meet those needs.

WorkSkills

1. According to the reading, if you are offered a job that does not meet your most important priorities, you should

   (1) not take the job unless you can meet your needs in a different way
   (2) take the job and start looking for a better one immediately
   (3) try to talk the employer into changing the job to meet your needs
   (4) take the job, but tell your employer you will not stay long

2. Which of the following factors is the most important in Ismael's situation?

   (1) earning more than $10 per hour
   (2) finding a job in a certain career
   (3) having a flexible work schedule
   (4) receiving health benefits

3. What two factors are most important in your own job search? Which is a higher priority? Explain your thinking.

   _____

   _____

   _____

   _____

RETAIL: Nelia needs to find work soon so that she can earn money to support her family. She would like to find a job working with computers. She can do word processing and create simple spreadsheets. She is also good at troubleshooting software problems. Her neighbor has offered her a job as a cashier at the hardware store he manages. Nelia isn't really interested in the work, but she thinks she could take the job for a few months and then look for something else. Her cousin advises her not to take a job unless she will work there for at least a year. **Do you agree with Nelia's cousin? Why or why not?**

_____

_____

Decide if a Job Is Right for You

Many people ask their friends if they know of any job openings. But few people ask themselves what it is they want from a job. To be happy in your work, you need to find a job that is consistent with your skills, interests, and desired **work environment.**

You have identified your skills, but now you need to ask yourself, "What skills do I most enjoy using?" For instance, you may be a very good driver, but do you enjoy driving enough to do it for a living? Think about which of your skills and talents you want to use on the job.

To help identify your interests, think about how you like to spend your spare time. Most people invest their free time in their interests. If you are interested in gardening, you may spend your time landscaping your yard, growing certain types of plants, looking through gardening books, or helping friends garden. You will be happier in a job that is closely related to your interests.

Your work environment can affect your satisfaction with a job. Some people like to work alone in a quiet office. Others enjoy interacting with co-workers and customers. Some people prefer working outside; others, behind a desk. Think about what kind of environment is best for you.

Prepare to Make a Commitment

When you accept a job, you make a commitment to an employer to do the best work you can. Hiring and training new employees is expensive for a company. Some employers estimate that it can take as long as six months for a new employee to be able to do all assigned tasks without help. Most employers want workers to make a commitment of at least one year.

There are many advantages to making a commitment to stay at a company at least a year. Once you thoroughly learn a job, you can begin to do your best work. As your employer gets to know more about you, your skills, and your work attitudes, he or she may give you opportunities to work up within the company. You may have a chance to take work-related classes and receive on-the-job training to gain new work skills. Your new work skills may bring salary raises and other benefits. And finally, if the time comes that you need to look for a new job, your employer will be willing to give you a good **recommendation.**

WorkSkills

1. In your own words, explain why it is important to commit to a job for at least one year.

   _____

   _____

   _____

   _____

2. Lena is an excellent typist and is good at office work. She also has experience using computers. Although Lena likes where she works, she is ready for new challenges and an opportunity to advance. To be happy with her work, Lena should

   (1) look for another typist job because she has a talent for it
   (2) stay away from office work entirely
   (3) explore work-related classes to gain new work skills
   (4) look for an office job that doesn't require computer use

COMMUNICATE

You can easily find information about careers, skills, and companies by visiting the public library or using the Internet. But how can you find out what it is really like to work in your career field? What are the job conditions? What are the best things about the job? What are the worst?

The best source of information about working conditions is an employee. Think of at least one person you know who works in a setting similar to one you think you would enjoy. Set up an information interview. **In your notebook or on a separate sheet of paper, prepare for the interview by listing ten questions that can help you learn more about life on the job.**

Comparing Job Opportunities

CONSTRUCTION: Kamaal is looking for a job with a future. He enjoys outdoor work and would like to work in construction. Kamaal has been offered a job as an apprentice concrete mason. The job pays $14.75 per hour with frequent chances to earn **overtime pay.** But Kamaal will be out of work when the weather is bad. The work is physically demanding, but Kamaal is in good shape. Once he joins the union, Kamaal will get health benefits. He will be trained on the job and will also learn about other jobs in the construction trades. Kamaal knows that the job outlook for concrete masons is excellent. As he gains more skills, he could easily earn up to $40 per hour. **Make a list of positive reasons why Kamaal should take this job.**

_____

_____

_____

Examine the Pros and Cons

Deciding whether a job is right for you can be a difficult decision. One way to evaluate a job opportunity is to try to see the good and bad results of taking a job. Positive factors are *pros,* or pluses. Negative factors are called *cons,* or minuses. Whether a factor is a pro or a con depends on your needs and your goals. For instance, having the chance to work overtime might be a plus to one person and a minus to another.

Organize Your Thinking

Many people make a chart to more clearly evaluate the pros and cons involved in making a life decision. One way is to draw a line down the middle of a sheet of paper. Label the columns *Pros* and *Cons.* As you list items on the chart, put related items across from each other like this:

PROS	CONS
• **Pay:** Good salary—$375 per week • **Hours:** 40 hours per week • **Benefits:** Good medical plan—HMO • **Location:** Close to home; could walk or take the bus	• No overtime hours • Occasional Saturdays • No dental plan • No work in bad weather • **Advancement:** No opportunities for raises until I have worked there for at least one year.

Weigh the Pros and Cons

How can you use the pros and cons to help you make decisions? First, you have to know how much weight to give each one in your decision-making process. For instance, if earning money is the most important factor for you, then a high wage would be worth more to you than a short commute.

One way to weigh pros and cons is to assign each of them a weight, or value. For instance, you could put check marks or stars next to each item, like this:

✔✔✔ **very important**
✔✔   **somewhat important**
✔   **not important at all**

Once you have weighed your pros and cons in this manner, add up the checks or stars. Which has more checks, the pros or the cons? If the pros have more weight, then it may be a good job for you.

Three check marks next to a pro mean a "strong positive," while three check marks next to a con mean a "strong negative."

WorkSkills

1. In your own words, what is the purpose of listing the pros and cons for each job possibility? Write your answer on a separate piece of paper.

2. When Kamaal weighs the pros and cons of the new job, he puts three check marks next to the con "No work in bad weather." The three check marks suggest this con is

    (1) an unimportant factor in deciding whether to accept the job
    (2) a very important reason to consider turning down the job
    (3) somewhat important to consider as he weighs his options
    (4) a very important reason to accept the job

3. Which of these statements is true about examining pros and cons?

    (1) A high salary is the most important pro for any job seeker.
    (2) It is best to wait until you have been offered a job to examine the pros and cons.
    (3) It is best to turn down any job with more than two cons.
    (4) A pro to one job seeker might be a con to another.

SERVICE: Silas would like to work in financing. He has some bookkeeping experience and has taken a few classes in investing. Silas hopes to get a job in a bank and work his way up. To learn more about what it is like to work in a bank, he decides to visit the banks in his area. At one bank, an employee in New Accounts asks if he needs help. Silas explains he would like to work in banking and is just looking for information. The employee offers to spend a few minutes during her break to talk to him about his career. **With a partner, brainstorm three questions Silas could ask to learn more about what it is like to work in a bank.**

_____

_____

_____

Find Out More About a Company

Suppose you have found a job opening that you want to pursue. The job has more pros than cons. Your resume is finished and you are ready to apply for the job. Before you submit your resume or schedule an interview, there is one more step you should take. You need to gather information about the company. This information can help you investigate further whether a job will meet your needs. It will help you answer questions during a job interview and even help you choose what to wear to the interview.

Do Library and On-Line Research

The public library is a good source for information about the size of a company and its predicted growth. You can also search magazine and newspaper indexes for articles about the company.

Many public libraries have computers that are hooked up to the Internet. Run a search for information about the company using the company name. You may find articles about the company's performance and its products, services, and advertising strategies.

Visit the Workplace

Most companies are public places, and you are a member of the public. Drop by the company lobby and look around. However, do not wander through the building unless you are escorted by an employee.

During your visit, be sure to notice how the employees dress. Look for displays describing the company's products and services. Pick up free brochures telling about the company.

Talk to Employees

The best way to gain information about what it is like to work at a company is to talk to an employee. If you don't know anyone who works there, call some of the people in your network. A friend, an instructor, or a former employer may be able to refer you to a company employee.

. . . .

WorkSkills

1. Silas wonders if Home Bank has offices in other cities. How could he find out this information? Suggest two ways.

   _____

   _____

Write *True* if the statement is true; *False* if it is false.

_____ 2. If you are not actually a customer, you always must have permission to visit a company.

_____ 3. Having information about a company ahead of time will not help you during the job interview.

_____ 4. The best way to find out what it is like to work at a company is to do research at a public library.

_____ 5. To find out about a company's dress code, you could visit the company or ask an employee.

MATH MATTERS

. . . .

Another important area of research is to estimate the cost involved in taking a certain job. Think about the kind of job you would like to have. Then make a list of the expenses you will have if you get the job. Will you need to buy a uniform or special tools? Will you need to pay union dues? Will you have additional transportation, child care, and food expenses? Compare these costs with the salary you expect to earn. **Will your salary cover the costs of your new job as well as your basic needs? On a separate piece of paper, write a paragraph explaining how you reached an answer.**

Review

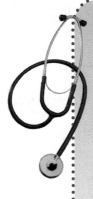

HEALTH CARE: Kina has worked 35 hours per week at the East Winds Cafe as a food server since May 1996. She takes customers' orders, serves their food and beverages, prepares their bills, and sometimes accepts payments. On certain days, she also seats customers and sets up and clears tables. She works the lunch and dinner shift five days a week and earns about $265 per week, including her tips.

Kina wants to get a job in health services. She attends City College and has been taking courses to become a medical assistant. As soon as possible, Kina would like to find a full-time job in the health field. If necessary, she could continue her studies at night. She would like to find a job that has health benefits and pays at least as much as she earns at the cafe.

One of her instructors tells her about a full-time nurse's aide opening at Valley Hospital. Pam Larsen, the personnel specialist who is interviewing job applicants, is looking for someone who is dependable, patient, and has a desire to help people. The job pays $7 per hour. Employees receive on-the-job training and can apply for health benefits after they have worked three months. To apply for the job, Kina needs to submit a resume.

1. Write an entry describing Kina's job at the cafe for the *Work Experience* section of her resume.

_____

_____

_____

_____

2. Compare the job at the hospital to Kina's career goals. Based on what you know about Kina, do you think the job meets her needs? Explain your thinking.

_____

_____

_____

_____

3. How could listing the pros and cons of taking the nurse's aide job help Kina decide whether to apply for the job?

_____

_____

_____

_____

Interviewing

OBJECTIVES

In this lesson, you will work with the following concepts and skills.

1. Understanding the interview process
2. Preparing for an interview
3. Learning appropriate ways to follow up after an interview

The video program you are about to watch shows you what part the interview plays in the hiring process. You will learn what an employer looks for during an interview and how to make a good **impression.** The program will also explain how the interview process can help you learn more about the job and the company.

As you prepare for an interview, you will need to practice giving answers to the most frequently asked questions. The video program will help you plan effective answers. You will also see how dress, **body language,** and word choices can affect the impression you make on an employer.

After an interview, you may need to follow up with a phone call or a letter. The video program will show you how to follow up an interview to your best advantage. You will also learn how to analyze your interview experience by thinking about what went well and what you would do differently next time.

Sneak Preview

This exercise previews some of the concepts from Program 5. After you answer the questions, use the Feedback of page 85 to help set your learning goals.

RETAIL: Warren is interviewing for a sales clerk job at a sporting goods store on a Monday morning. His interviewer is Dave Kimball. A portion of his interview is shown below.

Dave: We were very impressed with your resume, Warren. Why don't you tell me a little more about yourself?

Warren: I've always been interested in working in sales. I have been told that I am a good communicator, and I do have a genuine interest in helping people. I also love sports. I played soccer in high school, and I play on a city league softball team. I believe I could confidently help your customers choose the right sports equipment for their needs.

Dave: I see you worked at AJ Sports in the shoe department. Why did you leave that job after only six months?

Warren: The job was actually a temporary job. I was hired to work the holiday season from October to December, but they were happy with my work and kept me on for three more months.

Dave: Do you have any questions for me?

Warren: Yes. Do you have opportunities for advancement within your company? I would be very interested in someday working in a management position.

Dave: Actually, we have a fairly extensive management training program. Some of our sales associates have worked their way up to a management position. Thanks for coming in, Warren. I hope to make a decision by the end of the week.

Answer these questions based on the situation described above.

1. Why does Dave ask an open-ended question like "tell me about yourself"?

   (1) Dave is not well prepared for the interview.
   (2) Dave wants to find out more about Warren and his work attitudes.
   (3) Dave wants to make Warren feel less nervous.
   (4) Dave wants to check the accuracy of the facts in Warren's resume.

2. Give two examples from Warren's answers that show he would be good at this sales job.

_____

_____

3. Warren hopes he will not have to work on weekend evenings. Why would it have been a poor choice for him to have asked about days off?

_____

_____

4. Which of these would be an appropriate way for Warren to follow up on the job interview?

    (1) Stop by the office the next day to see if Dave has made a decision.
    (2) Call Dave if he has not contacted Warren by the end of the week.
    (3) Send Dave a gift thanking him for the interview.
    (4) Talk to the employees in the store to see if they have heard anything.

Feedback

- If you got all of the answers right . . . you have a foundation for going on job interviews and following up appropriately. As you go on interviews, think about how to present your skills and strengths with confidence.

- If you missed question 1 . . . you need to learn more about the purpose of the interview process and the way it is used by employers to screen job applicants.

- If you missed question 2 . . . you need to learn how to answer common interview questions and emphasize your skills and strengths.

- If you missed question 3 . . . you need to learn what types of questions to ask during an interview.

- If you missed question 4 . . . you need to learn appropriate ways to follow up on a job interview.

....

Answers for Sneak Preview:
1. Choice (2)   2. Any two of the following: He is a good communicator, loves to help people, loves sports, has sports experience, and expresses interest in a long-term commitment.   3. Asking about days off communicates a lack of concern for the employer's needs.   4. Choice (2)

Vocabulary for *Interviewing*

body language   communication through hand gestures, posture, and facial expressions

conservative clothing   clothes appropriate for the workplace. Conservative clothing is attractive but doesn't stand out in a flashy way.

expectations   outcomes that a person hopes will occur

feedback   information that helps a person evaluate how well he or she communicated or performed on a certain occasion, such as a job interview

follow up   to take steps to stay in contact with a potential employer after the job interview

impression   the feelings someone has about an individual after meeting him or her. The effect someone has on someone else.

posture   how a person positions his or her body when standing, sitting, or walking

sick leave   an amount of time that an employee is allowed to miss work for reasons of illness without losing pay

tone   the attitude and emotions an individual communicates in his or her choice of words and in the sound of his or her voice

PBS LiteracyLink®

Now watch Program 5.

After you watch, work on:
- pages 87–100 in this workbook
- Internet activities at www.pbs.org/literacy

AFTER YOU WATCH

program **5**

Interviewing

On the following pages, you will learn more about the ideas discussed in the video program and have an opportunity to develop your skills.

Think About the Key Points from the Video Program

To understand the interview process, you need to:
- Think about job interviews from the employer's viewpoint.
- Think about how you can use a job interview to learn more about the job and the company.

Learn what makes an interview a good one.

As you prepare for a job interview, you need to:
- Practice answers to commonly asked questions.
- Plan questions to ask the interviewer.
- Think about how to make a good impression.

As you go on job interviews, you need to:
- Think about how you can use the interview process to your advantage.
- Understand how the job interview fits into the hiring process and think about what will happen next.
- **Follow up** after the interview in appropriate ways.

Exploring the Interview Process

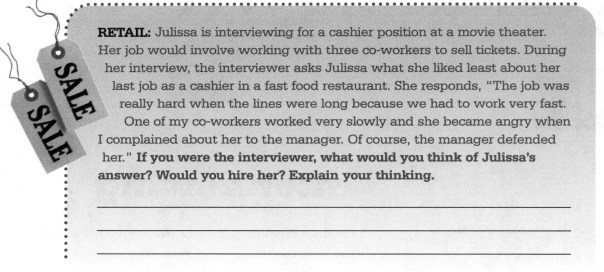

RETAIL: Julissa is interviewing for a cashier position at a movie theater. Her job would involve working with three co-workers to sell tickets. During her interview, the interviewer asks Julissa what she liked least about her last job as a cashier in a fast food restaurant. She responds, "The job was really hard when the lines were long because we had to work very fast. One of my co-workers worked very slowly and she became angry when I complained about her to the manager. Of course, the manager defended her." **If you were the interviewer, what would you think of Julissa's answer? Would you hire her? Explain your thinking.**

_____

_____

_____

You have already seen how employers use job application forms and resumes to gather information and screen applicants. Applicants who make it through this screening are given interviews.

The interview is the final step in the hiring process. Employers use the information gathered during the job interview to choose the best person for the job.

Learn How Employers Use Interviews

A job interview gives the employer a chance to meet you and gain a sense of what it would be like to work with you. During an interview, you will answer questions about your skills, experiences, and training, but the employer will be listening for much more than facts about you. The employer is listening for your personal qualities, attitudes about work, and communication skills.

Employers ask open-ended questions at job interviews to encourage you to talk openly. As you talk, the interviewer looks for clues that will reveal whether you will be happy on the job and committed to doing your best.

Learn How the Interview Can Help You

The job interview is a chance for you to put your best foot forward. Listen carefully to learn more about the requirements of the job and the **expectations** of your potential employer. Do your best to make a good impression. Try not to give the interviewer any reason to screen you out.

During your interview, don't make critical comments about a previous employer or co-worker. Even if your point of view is correct, your interviewer will probably react negatively.

Focus on the positive. Use every question during the job interview as an opportunity to talk about your skills and strengths. If you are asked directly about a weak area in your skills or work experience, take responsibility and talk about how hard you have worked to overcome the problem.

WORKTIP

To make a good impression with your appearance:

- Choose **conservative clothing** and jewelry.
- Make sure your hair, teeth, and fingernails are clean. Use deodorant.
- Make sure your clothes are clean and ironed and your shoes are clean and polished.
- Wear very little perfume or after shave.
- Wear minimal makeup.
- Do not chew gum or smoke.

WorkSkills

1. For the employer, the main purpose of the job interview is to

    (1) check the accuracy of information on the applicant's resume
    (2) find out how much the applicant expects to earn
    (3) gain information about an applicant's work attitudes and communication skills
    (4) inform the applicant about work schedules and benefits

2. Paul is interviewing for a job in an office. The interviewer asks, "What are your long-range career goals?" Paul responds, "I haven't made definite plans. I may move to Chicago if my girlfriend gets a job there. But that probably won't happen." Is this a good answer? Explain your thinking.

    _____

    _____

    _____

3. Think about Julissa's situation (page 88). How could she have answered the interviewer in a more positive way? Write a sample answer.

    _____

    _____

    _____

CONSTRUCTION: Alan is preparing for an interview for a job as a highway maintenance worker. He knows that employers often ask applicants to talk about their background. Alan plans to tell a little about his family and where they are from. He also plans to mention that he has a brother and an uncle who work in the construction industry. **What do you think of Alan's answer? How would you improve it?**

_____

_____

_____

_____

Think About the Ideal Interview

Take a few minutes and imagine what the ideal job interview would be like. In the ideal interview, the employer knows the requirements of the job and has prepared a list of questions that will encourage you to talk about your skills and strengths.

You are confident and relaxed. You have dressed appropriately to make a good impression and have arrived on time. After introducing yourself to the receptionist, you take a seat and patiently wait for your turn to be interviewed. You have come prepared with any information you may need to answer questions or fill out forms. You have a copy of your resume ready in case the employer asks for it.

Before coming to the interview, you researched the company and learned something about its products and services. Now, as you wait, you review your research and your goals for the interview.

When the interviewer approaches, you stand up and shake hands. You remember to smile and speak clearly. During the interview, you answer questions truthfully and talk about how your skills and strengths can help the company achieve its goals. You look the interviewer in the eyes as often as you can. Eye contact communicates that you are honest and confident.

You have also prepared one or two questions to ask the employer about the job, and the employer is glad to answer your questions. At the end of the interview, you have a sense of where you stand in the hiring process. Before leaving the interview, you find out when the employer will be making a decision. You have now gathered the information you need to decide whether this is the right job for you, and you have a clear understanding of what follow-up steps you will need to take.

Use an Interviewing Strategy

On an interview, you can't control what questions the interviewer will ask, but you can control what information you give in your answers.

Think about these common interview questions:
- "What are your skills and strengths?"
- "Why are you the right person for the job?"

The answers to these questions make up the range of information that you need to give the interviewer. Whatever you are asked, make sure you focus on the skills, strengths, and personal qualities that make you the right person for the job.

. . . .

WorkSkills

1. As you wait in the lobby for your interview to begin, you should

    (1) read a magazine or do a crossword puzzle
    (2) start a friendly conversation with the receptionist
    (3) review your research, skills, and goals for the interview
    (4) walk around the lobby and introduce yourself to others

Write *True* if the statement is true; *False* if it is false.

_____ 2. If you have already mailed your resume to the employer, you do not need to bring another copy of it to the interview.

_____ 3. An employer may look for clues such as making eye contact to decide whether you are giving honest answers.

_____ 4. As you answer interview questions, you should try to call positive attention to your work skills and strengths.

COMMUNICATE

Although you may have a good idea of your skills and strengths, you may be surprised to learn that other people may have a different point of view. Your friends and family may see different strengths and weaknesses. Learning how others see you can broaden your view of yourself and improve your ability to communicate your strengths during an interview. **Ask three friends or family members what they think is your greatest strength. Record their answers in your notebook or on a separate piece of paper. Think about how you can use this information on a job interview.**

Preparing for an Interview

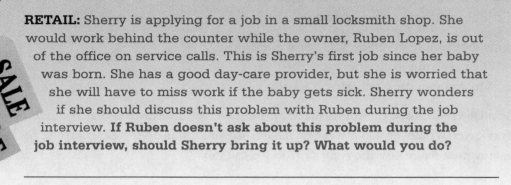

RETAIL: Sherry is applying for a job in a small locksmith shop. She would work behind the counter while the owner, Ruben Lopez, is out of the office on service calls. This is Sherry's first job since her baby was born. She has a good day-care provider, but she is worried that she will have to miss work if the baby gets sick. Sherry wonders if she should discuss this problem with Ruben during the job interview. **If Ruben doesn't ask about this problem during the job interview, should Sherry bring it up? What would you do?**

_____

_____

_____

A job interview is a kind of performance, and as in any performance, you will benefit from rehearsing. Look at the list of commonly asked interview questions. You can answer most of the questions by describing your skills and strengths. Use these questions to practice your interviewing skills.

Commonly Asked Interview Questions
- Tell me about yourself.
- What are your strengths?
- What are your weaknesses?
- Why do you want to work for this company?
- Why should we hire you?
- What did you like best about your last job?
- What did you like least about your last job?
- Describe your education. What skills have you gained?
- What are your career plans for the future?
- Why do you want to leave your present job?
- What motivates you to work hard?
- What kind of boss would you like to have?

Write answers to the more difficult questions. Then practice delivering your answers in front of a mirror. Use eye contact and good **posture.** Avoid slang and other kinds of informal language. When you feel comfortable, have a friend or family member give you a practice interview.

Remember that employers listen for more than the content of your answers. They also listen for clues in your **tone** or communication style that may reveal more about your personal qualities and attitudes. Make positive statements that emphasize your interest in being a success on the job. Avoid complaining or blaming your weaknesses on others.

Think About the Purpose of the Question

From time to time, you may be asked a question that doesn't seem to relate to the job. When you are asked an unusual or a difficult question, think about the reason behind the question. Try to understand the employer's concerns before you answer the question.

For example, suppose an employer asks whether you will mind commuting every day. Before you answer, try to imagine the employer's reason for asking the question. Perhaps the employer is concerned about your getting to work on time. You might answer, "It won't be a problem. I have reliable transportation, plus public transportation is also an option for me. You can count on me to be on time to work each day."

WORKTIP

To use body language to your advantage:

- Use good posture. Sit up straight but comfortably.
- Make frequent eye contact with the interviewer.
- Don't let your eyes wander to things in the room or on the interviewer's desk.
- Avoid nervous movements with your hands, such as twisting a ring or clicking a pen.
- Keep your hands quietly in your lap.
- Smile and look pleasant.

WorkSkills

Ruben asks Sherry, "Why do you want to work here?"

Sherry answers, "Now that my child is old enough, I want to get back to work. I enjoy learning how things work and solving problems. I also like helping people. I realize that when people call a locksmith, they think of their situation as an emergency. I am patient with people and know I could do a good job of calming them and assuring them that we would handle their problem as quickly as possible. I am also interested in working for a small company so that I can learn more and do a variety of tasks. I believe that working here would be just the challenge I need."

1. What personal qualities does Sherry's answer communicate?

   _____

   _____

   _____

2. How would you describe Sherry's work attitude?

   _____

   _____

   _____

MANUFACTURING: Varsik is interviewing at ABI Electronics for a job as a parts inspector. She would be using a magnifying instrument to make sure electronics components have been assembled correctly. Varsik thinks the employer is impressed by her work history and attitude. She is very interested in working for this company, but she is concerned about the work schedule. It will be difficult for her to work overtime hours unless she makes arrangements in advance. When the interviewer asks if she has any questions about the job, Varsik wonders if she should ask about overtime hours. **Is this a good time to ask about overtime hours? Explain your thinking.**

_____

_____

Plan Questions to Ask the Interviewer

During the job interview, employers usually expect applicants to ask a few questions about the company or the job. If you don't have any questions, the interviewer may assume that either you aren't interested in the job or you haven't learned enough about the company to know what to ask.

The questions you ask become part of the overall impression you make during the interview. Choose your questions carefully to show that you are concerned about the employer's needs as well as your own.

As you think about starting a job, you may be concerned about the health benefits the company offers or how soon you will start earning **sick leave** or vacation days. Although these are important things to find out, they are not appropriate questions for a job interview. Save these questions for your second interview with the company or until you've been offered a job.

Questions about vacation days or days off may suggest that you are more concerned about not working than being on the job. Generally, you should avoid questions that suggest you may have trouble getting the work done. On the other hand, if you do have definite schedule requirements, you should tell the employer during the interview process.

The following questions are good choices:
- Are there opportunities to advance within the company?
- How would I be trained for this job?
- What are the most important skills I would need to do the job?
- What are the specific duties for this job?
- How would my work be evaluated?
- What are the hours for the job?

Ask When a Decision Will Be Made

If, by the end of an interview, the employer has not already explained the next steps in the decision-making process, this is the time to ask. Before you leave the interview, you need to know what the employer plans to do next and what you are expected to do.

These questions can help:
- When will you be making a decision?
- Do you mind if I call on _____?

Plan to call the office the day after the employer plans to make the hiring decision. Meanwhile, continue your job search.

WorkSkills

1. In your own words, why is it important to prepare one or two questions to ask the employer during the interview?

   _____

   _____

2. If the employer does not tell you when he or she will be making a decision, you should

   (1) ask before you leave the interview
   (2) call the office later that day
   (3) call in one week's time
   (4) do nothing until you hear from the employer

COMMUNICATE

When you talk, less than 10 percent of your message is communicated through words. Most of what you communicate comes through your body language, voice, and tone. Try this exercise to improve your communication skills.

On a slip of paper, write three personal qualities that you want to communicate to an employer. Then have a friend ask you these questions: "What are your career goals?" and "What motivates you to do your best?"

Answer the questions as you would in an interview. Try not to mention the three qualities directly. Then show your friend your list and ask for **feedback** on how well you communicated these qualities. Ask for feedback on your verbal answer and your body language.

Interviewing and Follow Up

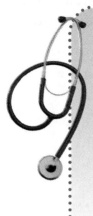

HEALTH CARE: Robin is interviewing for a position in a hospital kitchen. She would be helping to prepare food trays for patients. At the beginning of the interview, Robin feels nervous. The interviewer, Lovita Reynolds, asked if Robin had taken any nutrition classes in high school. Robin said "No," but later in the interview Robin remembered that her health class covered the subject of nutrition in some detail. Robin wonders if she should bring that up now that the interview is almost over. **What would you do in this situation? Why?**

_____

_____

_____

Help Yourself During the Interview

Most people feel nervous before a job interview. Feeling stress in a new situation is normal. In fact, even the employer may feel a little nervous. Both of you are meeting someone new, and both have important decisions to make. Feeling nervous is not bad; in fact, it can help you do better. Stress can focus your attention and sharpen your concentration. Do your best to relax, but don't worry if you feel a little nervous.

Employers will want to hire you if they feel comfortable talking to you and if you have the skills and qualities needed to do the job. So your main task on an interview is to help the employer get to know who you are and what you have to offer.

To do well in an interview, you need to be a good listener. When the employer talks, listen for the main idea. Think about what the employer's concerns are. If you don't understand a question, ask for more information.

To communicate well, you need to make eye contact. If the interviewer smiles or nods in agreement as you talk, you know your answer is on the right track. If the interviewer's facial expression seems to say "I'm confused" or "I need more information," try to state your main point clearly and give details to support your answer. Sometimes you may need to go back and make clear or add to an answer you gave earlier.

Stay focused on your goal of selling your skills and strengths. Every answer should help the employer gain a greater understanding of your work attitudes, personal qualities, and job skills.

Avoid Unfair Discrimination

Not all discrimination is unfair. You discriminate when you choose which brand of soda pop to buy. You make your decision based on the drink's taste and cost. Employers also discriminate when they make hiring decisions based on an applicant's skills. This kind of discrimination is not against the law.

It is illegal, however, to make a hiring decision based on a person's race, gender, age, marital or family status, ethnic background, religion, appearance, or physical disabilities. Most interviewers are careful to avoid questions that ask for information that could be used unfairly against you. But you can help yourself by not volunteering information that may be used unfairly.

If you are asked an unfair question, you can refuse to answer it, but your best bet is to answer it and then turn the conversation back to your skills and strengths.

WORKTIP

To prepare yourself to handle difficult questions:

- Think honestly about what improvements you need to make in your skills or life situation to make you a better worker.
- Make a plan to make these improvements and write your goals on paper.
- If you are asked about a specific weakness during an interview, focus your answer on your plan to overcome it.

WorkSkills

1. In your own words, why is it important to make eye contact with the employer during a job interview?

   _____

   _____

2. On an interview, Alex is asked if he owns his own car. Alex knows owning a car isn't a requirement of the job. He thinks the interviewer may be concerned about his having transportation to and from work. Alex doesn't have a car. How should he answer the interviewer? Write a sample answer.

   _____

   _____

3. Which of the following reasons for not hiring an applicant is an example of illegal discrimination?

   (1) he does not have enough years of experience
   (2) she isn't strong enough to do the work
   (3) he is a member of a certain religious group
   (4) she cannot work on Sundays for family reasons

SERVICE: Janelle has interviewed for a job as a service repair person for an appliance manufacturer. If she gets the job, she would go to customers' homes to repair washers and dryers. The job pays well and she knows that the company has several openings. Janelle is very excited about this job. The interviewer told her that the company would not be making a decision for three weeks. Janelle has decided not to apply for any other jobs until she hears from the appliance company. **What do you think of Janelle's decision? Explain your thinking.**

_____

_____

Understand What the Employer Does Next

After your interview ends, the employer will make notes about his or her impressions of you and your work skills. After all applicants have been interviewed, the employer will evaluate the applicants and rank them using numbers to show the first choice, second choice, and so on, for the job.

Then the employer begins calling references for the top few applicants to verify information on the job application form and resume and to find out more about the applicant's attitudes and work habits.

In a small company, the employer may make a job offer to the top applicant at this point. In a large company, the employer usually invites several applicants back for a second interview. Employers may give skills tests at this time.

During the second interview, the employer will discuss pay, benefits, work schedule, and other specifics. If you are given a second interview, try to make a good impression and continue to focus on your skills and strengths. The employer may make a job offer soon after this interview.

If you don't get the job, the employer will usually notify you either by phone or by mail within a week or two. If you haven't heard from the employer within a reasonable time period, you may call the office, but don't make a pest of yourself by calling more than once or twice.

Follow Up After the Interview

While the experience is fresh in your mind, think about your interview. Keep a record using a notebook. Write down the name of the person who interviewed you and whether you need to do anything to follow up after the interview. Learn from the experience. Think about what you did well and what you need to do to improve. Your interviewing skills will improve with practice.

Continue the Job Search

Successful job seekers continue looking for a job even while they are waiting for a job offer. Although you may be very interested in a particular job, you improve your chances of getting a job when you increase the number of interviews you go on. You also improve your interviewing skills and gain knowledge about how much your skills are worth.

WorkSkills

1. Jim interviewed for a job on Monday. The interviewer said she would be making a decision within a week. Jim has a job interview on Friday, but he still hasn't heard from the first employer. Jim should

    (1) call the first employer on Friday morning to see if he got the job
    (2) cancel the job interview that was scheduled for Friday
    (3) notify the first employer that he will not be able to take the job
    (4) attend the job interview as planned

2. Janelle receives a call from the employer after one week. She is invited in for a second interview. According to the reading, in what ways will the second interview probably be different from the first? Write your answer on a separate piece of paper.

WRITE IT

Make a lasting impression by writing a thank-you letter after an interview. The letter need be no longer than two paragraphs. In the first paragraph, thank the employer for the job interview. Restate your interest in the job and summarize your skills and strengths. In the second paragraph, give your phone number, encourage the employer to call, and tell what you will do to follow up on the interview. **Study the model thank-you letter on page 184 in the Reference Handbook.**

Write a thank-you letter to an employer. You can handwrite your letter on stationery or a formal note card. Or you can type it on good quality paper using the spacing shown on How to Type a Business Letter on page 182. Check for errors. When you are sure the letter is perfect, sign it. You can use this letter as a model for writing thank-you letters in the future.

Review

SERVICE: Sadrac is interviewing for a job as a grounds maintenance worker for the city. His job duties would include mowing, watering, and fertilizing parks within the city limits. He would also help to maintain the city's soccer and baseball fields.

Sadrac is interested in gardening and landscaping. In high school, he submitted a landscape design for a new shopping center. He also completed a basic course in agriculture. Sadrac wants to pursue a career in landscaping someday. First, he needs to earn money for school and learn more about how to maintain lawns, trees, and shrubbery.

Sadrac knows that the interviewer is looking for someone who follows directions well, takes responsibility, and will commit to the job for at least a year. He knows he will have to learn how to operate some of the machines used on the job. He will have to learn more about safety practices. He has a driver's license and has experience driving a truck.

1. Paul Garrett, a worker in the city personnel department, is assigned to interview Sadrac. He begins the interview by asking, "Why are you the right person for this job?" Using the information above, write an appropriate answer for Sadrac to give Paul.

   _____

   _____

   _____

2. Paul seems interested in Sadrac's career plans. He asks him when he plans to go back to school and what school he is planning to attend. Why do you think Paul asked these questions?

   _____

   _____

   _____

3. Paul closes the interview by asking if Sadrac has any questions about the job. What are two appropriate questions that Sadrac could ask?

   _____

   _____

4. List two things Sadrac should do to follow up after the interview.

   _____

   _____

BEFORE you WATCH

program **6**

WATCH

Ready for Work

The video program you are about to watch will help you learn work habits and attitudes that will make you ready to do a new job. The program also will help you learn how to fit in at work and succeed on the job.

As you watch, think about what it means to be responsible. Both your employer and your co-workers will be counting on you to do your best. You will succeed on a job if you are on time, work hard without being told to, and put in a full day's work.

Once you have a job, you will be expected to overcome personal obstacles such as transportation problems or child-care problems. By setting goals and making plans in advance, your first days and weeks on the job will go more smoothly.

Sneak Preview

This exercise previews some of the concepts from Program 6. After you answer the questions, use the Feedback on page 103 to help set your learning goals.

MANUFACTURING: Dana has just been hired to work in a food packaging plant. On her first day on the job, her supervisor gave her a company handbook. In the handbook, Dana found this page.

c o m p a n y   h a n d b o o k

ACE packing

five ways
to
keep
your job

1. **Have a Positive Attitude:** You will do well at Ace Packing if you are willing to learn and willing to work. Valuable employees are those who follow instructions and are respectful to their supervisors.

2. **Be On Time:** Being late to work can be cause for losing your job. **Be punctual!**

3. **Get Along with Your Co-Workers:** You must have a good relationship with the people you work with regardless of differences in backgrounds and personalities. To win the respect of your co-workers, you must show them respect.

4. **Avoid Gossip and Complaining:** Do not spread rumors. Gossip can hurt your reputation and the reputation of others. Gossip and complaining can destroy work relationships. If you have a problem with something that happens on the job, talk to your supervisor.

5. **Be Honest:** Although you work here, you are not entitled to take free samples of products or take work supplies home for your own use. Be honest. Honest employees are valued, trusted, and often promoted!

Answer these questions based on the situation described above.

1. According to the reading, what are some behaviors that could cause workers to lose their jobs? Check all that apply.

    _____ **a.** not understanding a task the first time it is explained

    _____ **b.** spreading rumors about a co-worker or supervisor

    _____ **c.** missing a day of work because of illness

    _____ **d.** making a habit of being late to work

2. Dana forgot to bring notepaper for her class right after work. A co-worker suggests that she borrow a pad of paper from work. She could bring it back the next day. Is this a good suggestion? Why or why not?

    _____

    _____

3. After working the first day, Dana is concerned that she is going to have trouble getting along with her supervisor, Ruth Kelly. She had trouble learning to use one of the packing machines, and she felt that Ruth thought she wasn't trying hard. The best thing for Dana to do would be to

(1) talk to her co-workers about the way Ruth treated her
(2) complain to the manager about Ruth's attitude
(3) treat Ruth with respect and continue to learn the job
(4) try to avoid any dealings with Ruth

4. Dana drives her brother to school on her way to work. Sometimes the traffic near the school is bad, so Dana is worried about being late to work some mornings. To be work-ready, what should Dana do about this situation?

_____

_____

_____

Feedback

- If you got all of the answers right . . .

  you have a foundation for understanding what it means to be work-ready. Think about the impression you want to make on your first days and weeks on the job, and set goals to achieve success.

- If you missed question 1 . . .

  you need to think more about what an employer expects from a new employee.

- If you missed question 2 . . .

  you need to learn more about what kinds of attitudes and actions will help you succeed on the job.

- If you missed question 3 . . .

  you need to think about how you can form a positive relationship with co-workers and supervisors.

- If you missed question 4 . . .

  you need to think about your responsibility in making a plan to overcome personal obstacles.

....

Answers for Sneak Preview:

1. Choices b, d **2.** It is not a good suggestion. The handbook specifically says not to take supplies. If a supervisor sees her, she could lose her job. **3.** Choice (3) **4.** She should help her brother find another way to school or drop him farther away from the school or leave home earlier. In short, she should do everything she can to make sure that she will be at work on time.

Vocabulary for *Ready to Work*

criticism	comments that point out faults. *Constructive criticism* suggests ways to correct faults.
culture	the customs, beliefs, and work styles that characterize a company or work group
expectations	the skills and behaviors an employer hopes to find in employees
maturity	a state of development associated with being an adult. Mature workers consider the needs of their employer and co-workers as well as their own.
morale	a group's feelings about its responsibilities and challenges
obligations	actions required by an employer
persistence	refusing to give up. Working hard at something until it is achieved.
punctual	on time
qualifications	accomplishments that make a person well suited for a job

PBS LiteracyLink®

Now watch Program 6.

After you watch, work on:
- pages 105–118 in this workbook
- Internet activities at www.pbs.org/literacy

Ready for Work

On the following pages, you will learn more about the ideas discussed in the video program and have an opportunity to develop your skills.

Think About the Key Points from the Video Program

As a new employee, you will be expected to:
* Step in and perform the work as quickly and accurately as possible.
* Work hard to understand your responsibilities.
* Stay on the job long enough to have made the hiring worthwhile.

Once you are on the job, you need to exhibit attitudes and work habits that show that you are "work-ready."

This means:
* You are responsible and can be counted on.
* You are willing to learn.
* You can work well with others.

To get ready to succeed on a new job, you should:
* Set goals that will help you do your best right after you start.
* Make a plan for the first days and weeks on the job.

WORKTIP

To get along well with co-workers:
* Don't make problems for yourself by spreading rumors or complaining about your boss or a co-worker.
* Accept suggestions and **criticism** with a positive attitude.
* Don't offer suggestions about how co-workers could do their jobs better.
* Keep busy. Don't stand around and wait for someone to tell you what to do.

Understanding Your Employer's Expectations

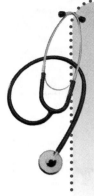

HEALTH CARE: You are the manager of a floor of a nursing home. The personnel department has hired Tal Alfaro as a new afternoon shift aide. You know that he meets the basic **qualifications** or personnel wouldn't have hired him. But you are concerned about whether he will have the personal qualities that will help him fit in and succeed on the job. **If you were Tal's supervisor, what types of personal qualities would you look for in a new worker on your shift?**

_____

_____

Have you ever had people come over to help you out with something? Perhaps you asked friends to help you move or get ready for a party. Maybe you asked friends to watch your children while you went out for a while. Think about what you expected from your friends. Was it important for them to be on time? Did you need them to make a strong effort? Certainly you had **expectations** of them.

Employers also have expectations of the people they hire. They spend time and money hiring and training new workers. They want things to work out. But they aren't willing to accept just any attitude or behavior.

To help yourself get ready to start a new job, you need to think about what an employer expects of a new worker. Take a minute to see yourself from the employer's point of view.

Get to Work on Time

The employer expects you to be at work on time—not fifteen minutes late, not even five minutes late. Being late can affect others. If you work as part of a team, not enough workers may be present to get the job done without you. Or your co-workers may have to do your work until you get there, and this isn't fair to them. In addition, customers may not get the services they need. This may cause your employer to lose business, and lost business means lost jobs.

Learn the Job Quickly

You may or may not have a training period when you start a new job. If you are doing a kind of work that you have done before, your employer may expect you to be productive from the beginning. If you are given special training, pay attention and learn the job as quickly as possible.

Get Along with Others

When you start a new job, you will meet some people you like right away. You will probably also meet people you don't like. That's natural. But remember that your employer expects you to be able to work well with *all* co-workers, supervisors, and customers.

Solve Problems

It would be wonderful if things ran smoothly all the time at work, but they don't. Production problems or difficult customers may cause problems. Sometimes things won't be explained well to you. Sometimes you will make mistakes. Your employer expects you to be able to solve problems yourself or take the initiative to get the help you need.

WORKTIP

During the first few days on a new job:

- Don't expect to master everything right away.
- You'll be getting a great deal of new information. Think about what information is most important to doing the job well.
- Expect to be tired at the end of the day. It's stressful to fit into a new environment.

WorkSkills

1. What qualities do employers expect of new workers? Check off all the qualities that apply.

   _____ **a.** like everybody that they work with
   _____ **b.** come to work on time
   _____ **c.** solve problems without asking for help
   _____ **d.** learn the job within a week's time
   _____ **e.** be productive in a short time period
   _____ **f.** work well with different types of people
   _____ **g.** solve a problem or ask for help with it

2. As Tal's new supervisor at the nursing home, you need to let him know your expectations. What would you say to him about being on time and working with others? Make a list of the points you would discuss with him.

   _____

   _____

   _____

   _____

   _____

RETAIL: Carrie has been hired to work in a large department store. Zuma Ramos, the floor manager, assigned Mona, a co-worker, to train Carrie. Today the store employees are taking inventory. Mona explained how to fill out the inventory forms, but Carrie wasn't sure she understood. When Carrie made a mistake on a form, Mona seemed impatient with her. Carrie told Mona that she hadn't explained the form well. At the end of the day, Zuma asked Carrie how her day went, and Carrie complained that Mona was hard to work with. Zuma talked to Mona about the problem. **If you were Mona, how would you feel about Carrie?**

_____

_____

If your career involves working with others, your job satisfaction will largely depend on the quality of your work relationships. Getting along with someone who has a different way of communicating or doing tasks can be difficult. But as a new hire, you must try to fit in as best you can. You need to work hard to get along with others.

Learn from Your Co-Workers

Your co-workers hold the key to your success. They have already solved many of the problems you will meet during your first few days. They understand the best ways to get the job done. If you make an effort to get along with your co-workers from the beginning, they will be willing to share their knowledge with you and to help you succeed.

Show respect for your co-workers. Thank them for their help. Try doing the job their way. They have more experience than you and have developed procedures that work. Although you may have done the job differently in the past or you may see a better way to do things, first try the job their way. As you gain their respect, you can suggest new ideas.

Be a Team Player

A team player plays to help the team win, not to gain personal success. In the workplace, you will never move up by tearing down someone else. Fault-finding and complaining will turn your co-workers against you.

Instead, show support for your co-workers. Don't place blame when a mistake occurs; work to solve the problem. Working to help others succeed shows **maturity** and is the mark of a leader.

Do Your Full Share of the Work

In a busy work setting, responsibilities often are assigned to a team of workers. As a member of a team, you must work hard so that other team members don't have to do your work for you. When one person continually lets the team down, resentment builds, team members no longer work well together, and work doesn't get done.

So work hard and keep busy. Look for work that needs to be done. Don't wait for a co-worker to do a difficult task. Step in and get the job done. Your co-workers will appreciate your efforts and be willing to support you.

· ·

WorkSkills

1. In your own words, why is it important to get along with your co-workers on the job?

    _____

    _____

    _____

2. Your co-worker shows you how to perform a task. You are sure there is a simpler way to do it. What should you do?

    _____

    _____

3. Nelda's boss asks her co-worker, Mark, to set up a new window display on Thursday afternoon. Mark feels sick and wants to go home early. Nelda should

    (1) explain to her boss that the display cannot be changed
    (2) help Mark by offering to set up the display herself
    (3) let the work go unfinished
    (4) complain to her boss

COMMUNICATE

You can learn a great deal from the experiences of others. Choose two friends or family members who have jobs. Interview them about their first day at work. Ask them what was the hardest thing about the day, what problems they encountered, and what they did to overcome them. Then ask if they have any advice for you. **On a separate piece of paper, write a paragraph summarizing their advice and ways you will apply it on the job. Share your summary with a friend or classmate**.

Learning the Meaning of "Work-Ready"

CONSTRUCTION: Ica recently started a job as a carpenter's assistant. During her 8-hour day, she gets two 15-minute breaks and a 45-minute lunch period. The first day she was late getting back to work after lunch because she had to make a phone call to arrange a ride home from work. The second day she was late to work because her morning ride was late. That afternoon, her supervisor warned her that if she didn't manage her time better, she might lose her job. Ica thinks the supervisor is unfair, because she has always had a good reason for being late. **What do you think? What advice would you give Ica?**

_____

_____

_____

When you accept a job, you are promising to put in a full day's work each workday. You are work-ready when you have accepted this responsibility and have committed to doing your best work every day.

Take Responsibility

A responsible worker can be counted on to come to work on time. Being late or absent can cause problems for your employer and your co-workers.

Many people do not understand the importance of using their time wisely. Breaks are designed to give you a mental and physical rest from your duties. If you use the time well, you should be able to return to the job with renewed energy. If you try to accomplish more on your breaks than the time allows, you will return to the job feeling tired and unable to focus on your work.

Plan to work hard your entire shift. Plan to come on time and stay until it is time to leave. Put in a full day of work.

Being responsible also means showing a positive attitude toward your job and communicating a positive image. Dress appropriately for the job. Make sure you follow your company's dress code. Use language appropriate for the workplace. Avoid jokes and remarks that could hurt people's feelings.

Unexpected problems will occur. Your car may not start, you may get sick, or your child-care arrangements may fall through. Despite your problems, make every effort to get to work. Too many absences, no matter what the reason, can cost you your job. If you simply cannot get to work, notify your supervisor as soon as possible.

Come Able and Willing to Learn

No matter how much you know about a job, you will probably need some training. To learn a new job, you will need the help of your co-workers. If you are work-ready, you are ready to learn and able to appreciate your co-workers' help in learning the job.

You will also need to listen carefully to your supervisor and be prepared to follow directions exactly. You may want to carry a small notebook and make notes about the steps to follow in accomplishing your job.

Always show respect for your supervisor and co-workers. Show appreciation for their criticism, and use their suggestions to improve your job performance. Stay focused on learning the job. Do not react emotionally to the manner in which someone teaches you or comments on your skills.

WORKTIP

To show initiative on the job:

- Keep busy.
- Look for work that needs to be done.
- If you don't know how to do something, ask for further instructions and help.
- Admit mistakes and learn from them.
- Return from breaks and lunch on time.
- Work until the end of your shift.

WorkSkills

1. On the last day of your first week on the job, your car doesn't start and you are late to work. Suppose you are explaining the situation to your supervisor. Which statement takes responsibility for the problem?

   (1) I'm sorry I was late, but when it's cold outside, my car doesn't always start.
   (2) I'm sorry I was late, but I couldn't do anything about it.
   (3) I won't be late again unless I have more trouble with my car.
   (4) I'm sorry I was late; I will make other plans to get to work in case I have a problem with my car.

2. Kent is working as a food server in a restaurant. He has been a food server before. But after Kent waits on his first customer, his supervisor says that Kent will have to make some changes. Kent knows he is good at his job. How should he respond?

   _____

   _____

   _____

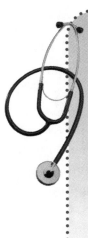

HEALTH CARE: Max has recently been hired as a medical receptionist. He works in a small urgent care clinic. People usually come to the clinic when they are very sick. Often, their regular doctors are unavailable. When there is a long wait, patients sometimes get upset. Max has worked hard all day. Several patients have complained about having to wait too long. One woman yelled at him and left the clinic. Afterwards, his supervisor, Raquel Lopez, criticized him for being unfriendly. She said he needed to be a better listener and show that he cares. **Max thinks he has been criticized unfairly. He feels angry. How should he respond to Raquel?**

_____

_____

_____

Control Your Emotions

There is an old saying that "the customer is always right." Obviously no one is always right, but on the job, you will gain little by proving that someone else is wrong. Whether you are dealing with a patient, a customer, a co-worker, or your boss, the best advice is to treat others as you want to be treated. Always think before you speak.

On the job, you must control your anger. If you disagree with a co-worker or your boss, wait to talk about it until you can discuss the matter calmly.

When you are ready to talk, try to see the other person's point of view. Starting from a position of "I'm right and you're wrong" destroys trust and only serves to make the other person angry too. Think about what the other person needs. When you are sure you understand his or her point of view, you are ready to be fair and talk about your own views.

Take Pride in Your Work

One reason to work is to feel pride in your accomplishments. Your job duties are important to your employer. If they are important to you as well, you will find satisfaction in your work. You will enjoy learning new skills and doing your job well.

Employees who take pride in their work improve the **morale** of their co-workers. Working as a team, co-workers do their best to avoid careless mistakes because they don't want to let their teammates down. As you strive to take pride in your work, you are developing important leadership qualities that will help you advance in your career.

Be a Problem Solver

Having a job will require some changes in your personal life. You will need to manage your time well so that you can put in a full day's work, get the rest you need, and take care of your family and other duties or **obligations.** You will need to plan ahead to take care of your clothes and appearance. You will need to solve any problems that arise.

Having a job brings many challenges, both on and off the job. With the right attitude, you will be able to overcome obstacles in your career path.

Problem solvers cope with difficulties by looking for creative solutions. They list the pros and cons of each decision and try to choose wisely. They ask others for advice and help. They are open to trying new ideas. Successful workers see problems as challenges that they can overcome.

WorkSkills

1. Melido works as a cook in a fast-food restaurant. Three times today he prepared orders wrong because Nita, the new counter worker, did not call the orders in correctly. Melido is angry that Nita's mistakes got him in trouble. How should Melido handle the problem? Write your answer on a separate piece of paper.

2. Which of these statements are true of problem solvers? Check all that apply.

    _____ **a.** Problem solvers look for new ways to approach a problem.
    _____ **b.** Problem solvers rarely ask for help from others.
    _____ **c.** Problem solvers plan ahead to avoid some problems.
    _____ **d.** Problem solvers often feel angry when facing a challenge.

WRITE IT

Employers often expect problem solvers to have creativity, **persistence,** and initiative.

Think of a time when you solved a difficult problem. You may have repaired a piece of equipment, helped to settle an argument, or weighed pros and cons to make a difficult decision. **On a separate piece of paper, describe the problem and your solution. Include details that show that you can be creative, persistent, and can take initiative.**

Working as a New Hire

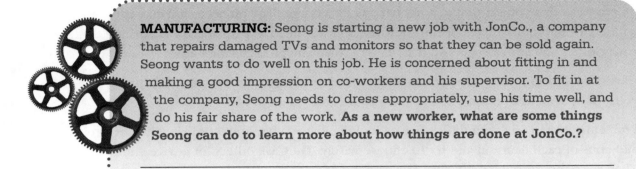

MANUFACTURING: Seong is starting a new job with JonCo., a company that repairs damaged TVs and monitors so that they can be sold again. Seong wants to do well on this job. He is concerned about fitting in and making a good impression on co-workers and his supervisor. To fit in at the company, Seong needs to dress appropriately, use his time well, and do his fair share of the work. **As a new worker, what are some things Seong can do to learn more about how things are done at JonCo.?**

_____

_____

You will need to learn many things when you start a new job. Of course, you will need to learn how to the do the job you were hired to do. But to succeed on the job you also must learn the **culture** or work style of a particular workplace. You need to understand how the workers dress, interact with each other, solve problems, and use their time.

Observe Others

Most businesses have employee handbooks to explain the company's policies about dress, vacation and sick leave, and health benefits. However, handbooks don't explain how to get along with co-workers and how to fit in. In addition, handbooks are sometimes outdated or even ignored. To find out what is actually expected of you, observe your co-workers.

Notice how your co-workers perform their jobs and how they interact with the supervisor. Notice how they dress and how they manage their time.

If you have worked in a similar job in the past, think about how the work style at your new job is different from your previous experience. Don't expect to convince your new co-workers to change their style to suit you. Instead, adapt to their way of doing things.

Make a Good Impression

During your first few days on the job, you will be meeting many new people. Do the best you can to learn the names of your co-workers. If a name is difficult to pronounce, ask a co-worker to say it for you; then break it into separate parts. When you have a few moments to yourself, make a list of your co-workers' names so that you can practice them after work.

You will probably feel a little nervous your first few days on the job. Your co-workers also may feel uncomfortable. They may be wondering whether they will like working with you. Show them you are easy to work with. Be open to learning new things. Don't be short-tempered or defensive if you make a mistake or ask a question they think is silly.

Once in a while, you may meet someone who is hard to like. You don't have to like everyone you work with, but you do need to have the maturity to get along with every co-worker. Do your best to be friendly and professional.

No matter what situation you find in your new workplace, do your best work. Put in a full day. If your co-workers do less than their share, let it go. It isn't your place to show them up. Simply make sure you do the job your employer has hired you to do.

> ### WORKTIP
>
> To help your co-workers feel comfortable around you:
>
> - Start a conversation about their interests. For example, if you find out that your co-workers like sports, ask what they think of a local team.
> - Ask for their help and advice about how to do your job. But, don't complain about the job or a supervisor.
> - Find out and talk about common experiences and interests that you share with a co-worker.

WorkSkills

1. What are two things you can do to make a good impression on your co-workers? Write your answer on a separate piece of paper.

2. On his break, Seong goes into the break room to buy a drink from the vending machines. A few of his co-workers are sitting at a table. One of the workers, Joe, is talking about a car he is rebuilding. Seong should

   (1) sit by himself until he gets to know his co-workers better
   (2) introduce himself and ask what kind of car Joe is rebuilding
   (3) bring a book to read during his breaks
   (4) stand by the drink machine and listen in on the conversation

3. Before lunch, one of Seong's co-workers gets into an argument with the supervisor. During the afternoon break, the worker and his friends gather in the break room and begin criticizing the supervisor. Seong is invited to join the group. What should Seong do?

   _____

   _____

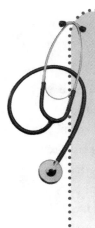

HEALTH CARE: Diane has started a new job as an aide at a hospital. Her first few days have been rocky. Her supervisor briefly explained Diane's duties, but has been out of the office since then. Diane gets along with a few of the other new workers, but the "old-timers" act as if she's invisible. She is so unhappy she wants to quit. But since she quit her last job after only two weeks, she wants to make this one work. **What are some reasons why Diane should stay on the job?**

_____

_____

_____

New jobs can be a challenge. You're learning new skills and procedures, even if it's a type of work that you've done before. You're also learning the expectations of a new employer, and you're getting used to being with a whole new set of people.

Some days you may feel like quitting, but if you quit one job easily, can you be sure that your next job will be any better? It is best to stay at a job for a while, even if it's not the ideal job. Most job situations can benefit you in ways beyond the money that you earn.

Develop Your Skills

Whenever you are in the workplace, you have the chance to develop your skills. You can develop transferable work skills that you can use on any job. You can also learn skills specifically related to a certain kind of work.

In addition, you can develop personal qualities that will help you in every area of your life. Every job opportunity gives you the chance to improve your communication skills and your problem-solving skills. Always look at every job as an opportunity to learn skills that you will need in the future.

Build Your Work History

Eventually, you will be looking for a new job. Most workers change jobs many times in their lives. When it is time to change jobs, one of the most important resources that you have is your work history. When you submit an application, an employer considers whether you would be a good investment. An employer wants to know:

- Does this worker have the skills that the job requires?
- Has this worker proven that he or she can stick with a job?

Develop a work history that shows that you have both the skills and the staying power for an employer to invest in.

Develop Your Network

How do people move ahead in the workplace? How do they find new jobs? As you have learned, one of the best ways to find new jobs is to network. Often you will hear about job openings from a co-worker or from someone you meet at work. Develop relationships with co-workers who will enable you to expand your future job search network.

WorkSkills

1. What are three reasons why you should stay with a new job?

   _____

   _____

   _____

2. What are some skills that you can develop on one job that will benefit you on other jobs in the future?

   _____

   _____

   _____

   _____

3. An employer is deciding between two workers who have basically the same skills. The employer will probably favor the worker who

   (1) lives closer to the workplace
   (2) has a history of staying with a job
   (3) heard about the job from a friend
   (4) wants to go back to school for more training

WRITE IT

Your friend who lives in Texas just started his first full-time job. You just heard from his sister that he's thinking about quitting the new job after only two weeks. **On a separate piece of paper, write him a short letter encouraging him to stay.**

- Start with a greeting. Dear _____:
- Make polite conversation. For example, ask how his life is going or how he likes living in Texas.
- Tell him what you heard from his sister.
- Give him two or three reasons to stick with his new job.
- Tell him to call you and let you know what he decides.
- End the letter with this closing: Sincerely, _____

Review

SERVICE: Rachel is starting a new job as a data entry clerk at Valley View Bank. Her supervisor, Matt Woodson, explains that her main duties will be data entry and typing loan application information to prepare loan documents for customers. She will also be asked to perform some general office tasks.

Matt gives Rachel an employee handbook and goes over her work schedule with her. He explains that she will work daily from 9 A.M. until 5 P.M. Her lunch break will be from 12:30 to 1:30 P.M. She will also have a 15-minute break each morning and afternoon.

Rachel will not help the bank's customers directly. Instead, she will be assisting the loan officers who must keep appointments with customers. Matt stresses that it is very important for Rachel to be at work on time so that the loan documents can be completed in time for each appointment.

Rachel is very pleased with the work environment at the bank. Her co-workers are friendly. She also knows that she needs to do good work in order to impress her supervisor.

1. On her third day at the bank, two of Rachel's co-workers invite her to come to lunch with them. After they eat, one of her co-workers wants to stop to run a short errand. Rachel is concerned that she will be late getting back to work. She has also noticed that the bank's employees are often late getting back from lunch and breaks. What should she do?

   _____

   _____

   _____

2. List three things Rachel can do to show Matt that she is work-ready.

   _____

   _____

   _____

3. Rachel works in a small office with Helen, another data entry clerk. Helen is talkative and takes frequent breaks. She interrupts Rachel often to tell her a joke or some office gossip. What are two goals Rachel could set to help her overcome the problems with Helen?

   _____

   _____

BEFORE you WATCH

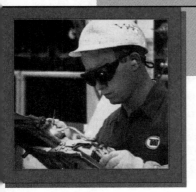

program **7**

WATCH

Workplace Safety

The video program you are about to watch will help you learn about safety issues in the workplace. More specifically, the program will help you spot potential **hazards** and understand your responsibility in creating a safe workplace.

Employers use a number of ways to keep workers informed about safety hazards. As you watch the video, think about the role *you* play in keeping safe on the job. For example, you can stay safe by watching for hazards, listening carefully to instructions, and reading the safety materials your employer has prepared.

On the job, your actions can place you or your co-workers at risk. If you follow every safety **procedure,** call attention to hazards, and use common sense, you can make the workplace safer.

OBJECTIVES

In this lesson, you will work with the following concepts and skills.

1. Exploring safety issues in the workplace
2. Learning about safety procedures on the job
3. Learning how to protect yourself and your co-workers from danger

Sneak Preview

This exercise previews some of the concepts from Program 7. After you answer the questions, use the Feedback on page 121 to help set your learning goals.

MANUFACTURING: Maggie works at an industrial bakery. The bakery makes bread and rolls that are delivered to grocery stores for sale. Maggie usually operates machinery on the bread production line, but sometimes she operates mixers and slicers. All the machinery is electrical. When Maggie started her job, she was shown how to work the machines and was given a safety manual. A page from the manual is shown below:

WORKING SAFELY WITH ELECTRICITY

Electrical hazards occur when electrical equipment is damaged and becomes "live." Equipment is said to be "live" when its metal parts carry electrical current. A worker who touches the metal will receive an electric shock.

Workers can prevent most electrical hazards by taking a few simple precautions:

- Read the instruction manual before using a machine for the first time.

- Inspect your machines at the beginning and end of your shift. If you observe frayed cords or damaged plugs or switches, report the problem immediately. Do not use the machine until you have inspected it.

- Do not operate machinery that has either a red danger tag or a yellow out of order tag. Tags are to be removed by supervisors only.

- Always shut down the machine at once when a problem occurs.

- Even if the problem seems small, do not try to fix the machine by yourself. Call your supervisor.

- If a machine is accidentally disconnected from a power source, turn off the machine before you reconnect the power.

- Electricity and water are a dangerous combination. Clean up spills immediately. Never operate machinery while standing on a wet floor.

- A machine that has been unplugged can still deliver a powerful electric shock. Do not attempt to disconnect the power and make repairs yourself.

Answer these questions based on the situation described above.

1. A mixer has large paddles that mix dough for bread. When ingredients are first added to the mixer, the machine slows down. One day the mixer came to a stop and made a loud hum. Maggie's co-worker suggested that she use a large metal spoon to stir the ingredients and get the paddles turning again. Should Maggie take her co-worker's advice? Explain your thinking.

_____

_____

2. On Tuesday, the supervisor asks Maggie to use a slicer. Maggie has never used the machine before. List two things Maggie should do before she turns on the power.

_____

_____

3. At the end of her shift, Maggie needs to clean the slicer. How can she find out more about how to clean it safely? Give three sources of information she could use.

_____

_____

_____

4. The floor under a mixer is wet from a recent mopping. A co-worker pulls a heavy cart of supplies behind the mixer and over its power cord. Afterwards, Maggie can see that the rubber casing on the cord has split open. What should she do?

(1) turn on the machine to see if it works   (3) move away from the wet area at once

(2) use tape to repair the split in the casing   (4) unplug the machine

Feedback

- If you got all of the answers right . . .   you understand how to recognize hazardous situations in the workplace. Think about how you will prepare yourself during the first few days and weeks on the job to understand all safety procedures.

- If you missed question 1 . . .   you need to think more about possible safety hazards.

- If you missed question 2 . . .   you need to learn more about how to apply safety procedures to create a safe work environment.

- If you missed question 3 . . .   you need to learn more about how to gather information about safety issues.

- If you missed question 4 . . .   you need to learn how you can protect yourself and your co-workers in a dangerous situation.

....

Answers for Sneak Preview:
1. No, she should shut down the machine and call her supervisor. She should not try to fix the machine by herself. Not only could Maggie damage the machine, but she could get hurt if the metal spoon conducted electricity. 2. Any two of the following: read the manual; inspect cords, switches, and plugs; check to make sure the machine is not tagged; ask a co-worker or her supervisor if she has any remaining questions. 3. The manual, her supervisor, co-workers who have used the machine. 4. Choice (3)

Vocabulary for *Workplace Safety*

chemicals	substances that are active ingredients in a product. In the workplace, chemicals are usually found in liquids, powders, and gases.
hazards	possible risks to safety or possible causes of an accident
incident report	a form that employees must fill out to report an on-the-job accident or injury. Also called an *accident report* or an *injury report.*
Material Safety Data Sheet	(MSDS) a list of information required by law to be provided for each product that contains potentially harmful chemicals
precautions	safety measures taken before a product or machine is used
procedure	a list of steps to be followed to accomplish a task. Safety procedures help reduce the risk of on-the-job accidents and injuries.
protective equipment	safety devices used by workers to reduce the risk of injury when handling chemicals or when using tools and machines. Protective equipment includes goggles, face shields, helmets, rubber gloves, noise protectors, and ear coverings.
regulations	government rules that are designed to protect people. Safety regulations ensure that companies take measures to keep their workers safe.
repetitive motion injuries	physical problems that are caused by repeating the same movement for a long period of time
ventilation	fresh air. Ventilation can be improved by opening a window or turning on a fan.

PBS LiteracyLink®

Now watch Program 7.

After you watch, work on:
- pages 123–136 in this workbook
- Internet activities at www.pbs.org/literacy

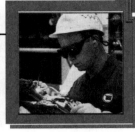

AFTER you WATCH

program **7**

Workplace Safety

On the following pages, you will learn more about the ideas discussed in the video program and have an opportunity to develop your skills.

Think About the Key Points from the Video Program

To stay safe on the job, you need to:
- Understand safety issues in the workplace.
- Recognize potentially dangerous situations.
- Create a safe work environment by following safety procedures and using common sense.

To meet your responsibility to prepare yourself to recognize safety issues:
- Listen carefully to training sessions on safety issues, and ask questions.
- Gather information by reading.
- Look for signs and other warnings about safety **hazards.**

To meet your responsibility to protect yourself and your co-workers:
- Learn what to do in an emergency or dangerous situation.
- Observe your environment for safety issues.
- Use common sense when handling **chemicals** and using equipment.

WORKTIP

As you learn to operate equipment and machinery:
- Make sure you understand the instructions you are given.
- Ask about safety features.
- Make sure you know where to find **protective equipment.**
- Ask what to do if a problem with the machine occurs.
- Make sure you understand how to turn off the power to the machine in case of an emergency.

Understanding Safety Issues

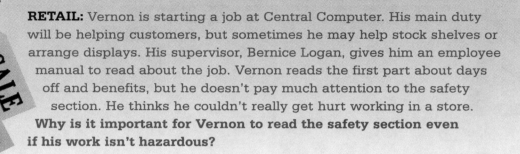

RETAIL: Vernon is starting a job at Central Computer. His main duty will be helping customers, but sometimes he may help stock shelves or arrange displays. His supervisor, Bernice Logan, gives him an employee manual to read about the job. Vernon reads the first part about days off and benefits, but he doesn't pay much attention to the safety section. He thinks he couldn't really get hurt working in a store. **Why is it important for Vernon to read the safety section even if his work isn't hazardous?**

_____

_____

Injuries are both painful and costly. If you are injured on the job, everyone loses. Your health and career may be permanently affected, your co-workers may have to work harder to do your share, and your employer may have to hire and train a new worker to take your place.

Plan now to read, understand, and follow all safety procedures on the job. It pays to work safely.

Stay Safe in the Workplace

Every job has certain risks. Accidents occur even in relatively safe jobs. Slips, trips, and falls are common causes of injury. Lifting improperly can cause back and neck injuries. Repeating simple motions also can cause injury.

Some jobs carry greater risks than others. For example, jobs that involve chemicals or machines can be especially dangerous if workers do not carefully follow safety procedures.

Some working conditions involve risk. Outdoor workers must guard against sunburn and heat stroke. Factory workers may need to wear ear protection to protect themselves from hearing loss. Workers who type, sew, or use certain machines all day long must guard against **repetitive motion injuries** by taking frequent breaks and using correct posture and hand placement as they work.

You will find different safety issues in different work environments. In the food industry, workers must be trained to use equipment safely, watch for food spoilage, and prepare food correctly to prevent the spread of disease. Manufacturing and construction workers must be trained to operate heavy machinery, work in hazardous conditions, and use potentially dangerous chemicals.

Find Potential Hazards

When you start a job, be aware of hazards. Look for trouble spots. Even an office job can have unsafe conditions. Be on the lookout for these common hazards:

- improperly used or stored cleaning chemicals
- an unclean environment
- poor lighting
- unclear pathways
- loud sounds
- broken furniture
- poorly maintained tools or equipment

Report a hazard to your supervisor at once. Do all you can to reduce the risk of injury. This may include warning co-workers of the situation, posting a notice near the hazard, or blocking off the area.

WORKTIP

When you use chemical supplies for the first time:

- Read the warning label before opening the container.
- If a label is missing, ask to read the **Material Safety Data Sheet.**
- Make sure you understand all first-aid procedures.
- Always wear the protective equipment required by your employer.

WorkSkills

1. List three safety concerns you could encounter in an office.

   _____

   _____

   _____

2. A customer's child spills a can of soda pop on the store's carpet. The manager asks Vernon to clean up the spill. He shows Vernon where to find a carpet cleaning solution. Describe two things Vernon should do before he uses the product.

   _____

   _____

3. In the Customer Service Department, two registers are close together in a small space. To reach his work station, Vernon has to step over the electrical cord from his co-worker's register. Vernon is concerned that he could trip on the cord. Vernon should immediately

   (1) stop working
   (2) make a sign to warn people about the cord
   (3) unplug the register
   (4) report the hazard to his supervisor

MANUFACTURING: Risa is starting a job in a print shop. She will be operating a small offset printing press. The press feeds paper through rollers that print the image on the paper. Risa's co-worker Carl is showing her how to use the machine. Carl explains that sometimes paper misfeeds. He shows her how he clears some jams without turning off the machine. "You will waste a lot of time," he explains, "if you turn off the power every time the paper misfeeds." A sign on the wall reads: "Always turn off presses before clearing paper jams." **Risa knows Carl has been assigned to train her, but she is concerned about his advice. If you were Risa, what would you do?**

_____

_____

_____

Create a Safe Work Environment

Employers have the responsibility of providing a safe work environment. They do this by identifying possible job hazards, getting rid of unnecessary hazards, and training employees to work safely. Employers also have the responsibility of following local, state, and federal government **regulations** about worker safety.

You have a responsibility to read and understand any safety materials you are given, pay attention to training, follow all safety procedures, and use common sense.

Understand Safety Procedures

A **procedure** is a series of steps that you can use to do a task safely. When you start a job, your supervisor and co-workers will explain the procedures your employer has developed. Safety procedures may be included in your employee handbook. They may also be posted on bulletin boards and near equipment.

In keeping with government **regulations,** you may also be required to take special classes. Safety training may be required before you can be allowed to operate certain kinds of machinery.

Make sure you completely understand the training you receive. Ask questions if instructions seem unclear to you. If you are asked to take a safety class, take it seriously. Workers who have been on the job for a while sometimes take shortcuts to save time. Never work unsafely. Always follow procedures to protect yourself, your co-workers, and the public.

Use Common Sense

Most jobs involve some risk. Your employer is responsible for protecting you from hazards, but it is impossible to protect you from all risks.

Use your common sense to avoid unnecessary risks. Many injuries take place near the end of a worker's shift. Workers who are tired and hurrying to finish sometimes take shortcuts or neglect to follow all safety rules. Don't make this mistake. Keep your mind on your work and don't rush.

After an accident, workers are often heard to say, "I had a feeling something was about to go wrong." Pay attention to your feelings. Get in the habit of checking your work area for hazards. If you recognize that a situation is dangerous, do something at once to remove yourself from danger or correct the problem.

WorkSkills

Write *True* if the statement is true; *False* if it is false.

_____ 1. It is against safety regulations for an employer to demand that you use unsafe equipment.

_____ 2. You may be required to take safety classes before you can perform certain parts of your job.

_____ 3. You have a responsibility to use common sense to reduce the risk of accidents.

4. In your own words, why is it important to follow all the employer's safety procedures?

_____

_____

WRITE IT

Think about the substances you have at home that contain chemicals. For example, you may have cleaning products, pesticides, or medicines. Choose a substance that could be harmful if misused. Read the directions and any warning labels on the product. **On a separate piece of paper, write a procedure—a list of rules—for handling the substance safely. Tape the procedure to the container or post it near the place where the substance is stored. Share your procedure with a classmate or friend to make sure your instructions are clear.**

Recognizing Safety Issues

CONSTRUCTION: Joe is an apprentice electrician. Yesterday, he was working with Alex, a co-worker, to install channels in masonry for wiring. The equipment used to cut through the brick made a lot of noise. By the end of his shift, Joe had a headache, and his ears were ringing. Joe asked Alex if they should be wearing some kind of ear protection, but Alex laughed and said that Joe would get used to the noise. **Joe wonders if he should mention the problem to his supervisor. What would you do?**

_____

_____

Employers need their workers' help to keep the workplace safe. By providing safety training, employers fulfill the requirements of the law and help workers recognize unsafe situations. By making you aware of potential hazards, employers lessen the chance that you will have an accident.

Think About Safety from the Start

During your first few days, your supervisor and co-workers will be helping you learn the job. Because there is so much to learn at first, safety concerns often take a backseat to learning how to do the job.

Make sure your supervisor and co-workers explain safety rules and procedures to you. As they explain each task, listen for safety concerns.

Ask Questions

During your training period, ask for help about the best way to do each job. It is appropriate and professional to ask questions. Your employer will appreciate that you are doing all you can to work safely.

Here are some examples of safety questions you may ask:
- How do I adjust the height of my chair or computer monitor?
- Are there carts for moving supplies?
- What is the procedure for reporting spills?
- Where are cleaning supplies kept? Am I allowed to use them?
- Where can I find reading materials and manuals about the machines and chemicals used in the workplace?
- Where is the protective equipment (goggles, gloves, etc.) kept?
- Where are safety rules and procedures posted?

Gather Information

Every piece of equipment comes with a manual. The manual explains how to operate the machine safely, maintain the equipment, and troubleshoot problems. Find out where these materials are kept and read through them at the earliest opportunity.

Each chemical product comes with a Material Safety Data Sheet (MSDS) that, according to federal law, must be kept on file. The MSDS explains what health hazards are caused by the chemical and what **precautions** must be taken before the chemical is used. The page also explains emergency and first-aid procedures, proper disposal of the chemical, and proper cleanup of spills.

If safety manuals or data sheets are missing, your employer can obtain replacements from the manufacturer. You can also search the Internet for safety information on various products and chemicals.

WORKTIP

Accidents often occur when workers are tired or are not paying attention. These tips can help you reduce your risk of injury:

- Make sure your work area has good **ventilation.**
- Drink plenty of fluids as you work. Water is best.
- Use rest breaks to change your pace. If you have been sitting all morning, take a brisk walk on your break.
- Get regular exercise before or after work.

WorkSkills

Greg works in a hotel kitchen. He has been asked to use a new product called CleanJet. The MSDS gives the following information.

HEALTH HAZARD DATA

EYES: Will burn and irritate. Flush with water for 15 minutes and get medical help if irritation continues.

SKIN: May irritate and cause blisters. Wash with water; apply antiseptic skin cream.

CONTROL MEASURES: Use in well-ventilated area. Use rubber gloves. Do not splash in eyes. Keep container closed when not in use.

SPILLS: Small spills can be washed to the sewer drain.

Greg accidentally kicks over the bottle of CleanJet in the food storage area. After warning co-workers to avoid the spill, how should Greg go about cleaning up the spill? Include any precautions he should take. Write your answer on a separate piece of paper.

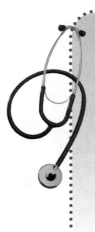

HEALTH CARE: Colin recently started working as a nurse's aide. He likes the work, but he thinks a lot of the procedures he is asked to follow are a waste of time. Even hand washing has a special 7-step procedure that is posted on the wall above every sink. Colin thinks the way he washes his hands is fine. He doesn't have time to follow seven steps after he helps each patient. **What do you think? How could Colin's attitude affect his job and his patients?**

_____

_____

_____

Read Postings

Employers post procedures to remind employees of the steps they should follow to do the work safely. When you start a new job, you should read all postings. Reading the procedures can help you learn a new job quickly.

After you have been on the job for a while, you may be tempted to skip steps in procedures to save time. Some steps may not make sense to you. You may think the procedures are there for new employees only. But this isn't true. Your employer has developed these steps to keep you, your co-workers, and the public healthy and safe. Follow the steps even if you don't see their value.

Recognize Warning Signs and Symbols

Government agencies have developed signs and symbols to warn workers about dangerous situations. Certain colors are used in every workplace to mark hazards. Understanding how to interpret these colors can help you identify potential risks.

Warning or danger signs always have a red or red-orange background. The word "Danger" is printed in a contrasting color, usually black or white. Below the danger symbol, there will be more information explaining the hazard. The following colors have special meaning in the workplace.

Colors	Meaning
white or black	housekeeping hazards
orange	physical hazards
green	first-aid and safety equipment
blue	caution against using unsafe equipment
red	danger, stop, and fire protection equipment
yellow	general caution

WorkSkills

1. Lee works in a child care center. The following sign is posted in the first-aid station.

> If rubber gloves are used for any reason, you must wash your hands immediately after the gloves are removed.
> The use of gloves alone will not prevent the spread of germs.

Lee puts on gloves to help a child with a nosebleed. Afterwards, she doesn't see any blood on the gloves, so she takes them off and goes back to work. According to the posting, why should Lee have washed her hands?

_____

_____

2. Maintenance workers are cleaning out a drain in the middle of a workroom floor. They use warning tape to mark off the area so that workers will not fall. What color of tape will they most likely use?

(1) orange
(2) green
(3) blue
(4) black

3. In your own words, why is it important to follow procedures exactly even if you do not understand their purpose?

_____

_____

MATH MATTERS

Some cleaning solutions must be diluted, or mixed with water, before use. Usually, the instructions give a ratio to indicate how much water to add to the concentrate. For example, if the instructions call for a 1 to 5 ratio, you should use one part of the concentrate and five parts of water. A part can be an ounce, a cup, or any other unit of measure.

A floor cleaning product must be diluted to a 1 to 8 ratio. How much water would you add to one-fourth cup of the concentrate? 6 fluid ounces? 2 teaspoons? Write your answers on a separate piece of paper.

Learning How to Protect Yourself and Your Co-workers

CONSTRUCTION: Mariana is working on a kitchen remodeling job. As a construction worker, she is responsible for providing many of her own tools and safety equipment. To finish installing the cabinets, Mariana needs to use an electric drill. Her boss's safety procedures require her to wear safety glasses, but she can't find hers. She may have left them on the truck. She needs to finish her work on the cabinets now, or she will hold up the entire project. Mariana has used a drill many times at home without wearing safety glasses, and she has never had a problem. **What would you do if you were Mariana?**

_____

_____

Every day, work situations occur that could become dangerous. Most accidents can be prevented by following safety procedures carefully and by using common sense. By making good decisions, you can protect yourself and your co-workers from unnecessary risks.

Know What to Do

All jobs have some risk. Employers can manage some risks by setting up procedures and training workers to follow them. But some risks are unexpected. When you find yourself in a hazardous situation, what can you do to stay safe?

One of the best ways to stay safe on the job is to be alert for possible dangers. When you are well rested and focused on your job duties, you are also more aware of hazards and unsafe conditions. Keeping your mind on your work is an important step in avoiding unnecessary risks.

Enroll in employee training courses at the first opportunity. Government regulations require most companies to provide safety training for employees. You may be offered classes in equipment operation, driving, food preparation, or basic health and first aid. You may also be required to take special courses that relate to your career. For example, workers in the health field are required to take a class to learn how to handle blood products in the workplace.

Signing up for these courses shows that you take your job seriously and that you are willing to learn. Your employer will appreciate your attitude and commitment to safety.

Check Your Environment for Safety

Did you know that accidents are more likely to happen in an environment that is familiar to you? As you get used to your environment, you are less likely to notice the hazards it contains.

Changes in the workplace can bring hazards. Make sure to put away new supplies properly. If you get new equipment, machinery, or chemicals, read the manuals and safety instructions before you use the new items.

If you see your co-workers performing their jobs in an unsafe manner, talk to them. If their behavior places others in danger, discuss the problem with your supervisor. Always put safety first.

WORKTIP

To reduce the risk of injury in an office:

- Make sure you have adequate lighting.
- Prevent slips and falls by keeping walkways clear.
- Clean up spills immediately.
- Use good posture and correct hand and wrist position when typing.
- Always follow correct procedures when lifting boxes or supplies.

WorkSkills

Write *True* if the statement is true; *False* if it is false.

_____ 1. Your employer is responsible for managing risks in the workplace.

_____ 2. You are more likely to be injured if you are not alert.

_____ 3. You may be required to take certain safety classes in order to do your job.

4. On a winter's day, the first workers to arrive track ice and snow into the building as they enter. Soon the snow melts. When you enter the building a few minutes later, you almost slip in the puddle of water. You have a responsibility to

   (1) put a warning sign in the break room
   (2) tell a supervisor about the hazard immediately
   (3) be more careful next time
   (4) tell the workers who made the mess to clean it up

5. The paper shredder in your office jams. One of your co-workers thinks she can fix it. She starts to pry the paper loose while the power to the shredder is on. You are concerned about your co-worker's safety. You should

   (1) report the problem to your supervisor
   (2) put a warning tag on the machine
   (3) look up the problem in the machine's instruction manual
   (4) tell your concerns to your co-worker at once

SERVICE: Rod is putting a new toner cartridge in his laser printer at work. As he takes the cartridge out of the box, it slips from his hands and hits the edge of the desk. The plastic cartridge breaks open and the black powdery substance goes everywhere. Rod has toner on his hands and clothes. He thinks he may have inhaled a small amount of the toner because he keeps coughing and sneezing. Rod doesn't want to report the accident to his supervisor. He is afraid he will get in trouble for dropping the toner or that his supervisor will think he is a sloppy worker. **Do you think Rod should report the accident? What would you do?**

_____

_____

Know What to Do If an Accident Occurs

Accidents do happen. Despite procedures to keep workers safe, problems arise. What should you do if you witness an accident? What is your responsibility if an accident happens to you?

As an employee, you have the responsibility to:

- Be aware of hazards.
- Read and understand safety procedures.
- Follow all safety rules.
- Use common sense to keep you and your co-workers reasonably safe.

When an accident occurs, don't panic. The first step in handling an emergency is to decide whether the situation is life-threatening. If the victim of an injury is having difficulty breathing, is bleeding, is unconscious, or may have injuries to the back or neck, call for emergency services at once and begin appropriate first aid.

Remember the A-B-C's of first aid. *A* stands for "open the airway." *B* means to "check the breathing." *C* means "check the circulation by taking the pulse." If someone is experiencing problems in one of these three areas, you must get help immediately.

If the injury is less serious, follow your company's procedures for getting help. Do not take action that would do greater harm to the individual.

If no one is injured, do you need to report the accident? Yes, you do. Every accident is an opportunity for your employer to take a good look at the company's safety procedures. If procedures are not working, they may need to be changed. At times, employers must develop new procedures.

Fill Out an Incident Report

Most companies require employees to report an accident or injury on an **incident report**. The forms are a record of the situation that caused the accident. The reports can be used to evaluate safety procedures.

To fill out an incident report, you will need to name the accident victim, the date and time of the accident, how it happened, and who witnessed the accident. You may also need to tell what action was taken to help the victim of the accident. The report is usually signed by the person writing the report, the witnesses, and the supervisor.

....

WorkSkills

1. In your own words, explain your own responsibility in keeping the workplace safe.

   _____

   _____

2. A co-worker has just suffered a serious cut on his hand. You witnessed the accident. The first thing you should do is

   (1) call your supervisor
   (2) find out whether your co-worker needs emergency help
   (3) find a first-aid kit
   (4) fill out an incident report

3. During a storm, you get a mild electric shock when you touch the metal casing on a piece of equipment. Although you were not injured, why is it important to report the situation to your supervisor?

   _____

   _____

   _____

COMMUNICATE

A friend at work has been staying up late to study for an important test. Lately, you notice that your friend has been very sleepy during the day. You are concerned about your friend's safety. You decide to talk to your friend about the importance of being alert on the job.

Think about what you would say to your friend. On a separate piece of paper, list the important points you would choose to communicate.

Review

MANUFACTURING: James works in a warehouse. His employer is teaching him how to operate a forklift safely. A forklift is a kind of industrial truck that is used to carry and stack heavy loads. The items to be carried are secured on wooden pallets that fit onto the forks on the front of the forklift.

On the first day of his training, James is given the following information.

ALWAYS WORK SAFELY!

- Never stand or work close to a moving forklift.
- Position loads evenly on the pallet to prevent forklift overturns.
- Do not make sharp turns or drive near other vehicles or objects.
- Keep your head, arms, and legs inside of the cab at all times.
- Wear seat belts and body restraints while inside the cab.

James's boss explains that most injuries occur when a forklift tips over. He tells James the safest place to be if a forklift overturns is inside the cab. James should never try to jump clear of the vehicle.

1. Before James operates the forklift to move a load, he should make sure the situation is a safe one. Name three safety issues James should check before he operates the vehicle.

   _____

   _____

   _____

2. A guard designed to protect the worker from the movement of the wheels is missing from one wheel. If James wanted to find out more about the need for the guard, what could he do? List two sources of information.

   _____

   _____

3. James will be moving several pallets of supplies from the loading dock into the warehouse for storage. A few of his co-workers are taking a break on the loading dock. James is concerned about their safety. What precautions should he take?

   _____

   _____

   _____

program **8**

Learning at Work

The video program you are about to watch will help you learn your new job quickly. You will see how to manage your learning and how to make choices that can help build work skills for the future. The program also will help you handle the large amount of information you will receive during that first week on the job.

As you watch, think of ways you can learn to do your job. Successful employees take responsibility for their own training. Be ready to use all ways available to you to "learn the ropes."

One important skill that you will need is the ability to distinguish between things that must be handled immediately and things that can wait for a later time. The video will show you ways to **prioritize** the expectations of your employer successfully.

Sneak Preview

This exercise previews some of the concepts from Program 8. After you answer the questions, use the Feedback on page 139 to help set your learning goals.

HEALTH CARE: Emilio has a new job as a laundry aide at Woodson Retirement Center. On his first day, the housekeeping supervisor, Donna, explains that Emilio will learn how to perform his duties through on-the-job training. To begin his training, she gives him the following page:

W   **WOODSON RETIREMENT CENTER**

JOB: Laundry Aide

REPORTS TO: Housekeeping Supervisor

SUMMARY
Laundry aides prepare and deliver linens to the various departments at the retirement center. Laundry aides must be courteous to residents living at the center, able to follow directions, and able to handle interruptions.

RESPONSIBILITIES
1. Perform assigned laundry tasks.
2. Collect, sort, wash, and dry the clothing of the residents.
3. Sort, wash, and dry soiled linen used by various departments.
4. Fold clean linen by hand.
5. Clean laundry equipment and area.
6. Deliver clean laundry as assigned.
7. Take good care of residents' possessions.
8. Keep information about residents confidential.

PERSONAL QUALITIES
1. Good physical and mental health
2. Ability to understand and follow directions
3. Good hygiene and appearance; keeps uniforms clean and in good repair
4. Initiative and good judgement
5. Willing to learn
6. Friendly and polite to co-workers and residents

EMPLOYEE HANDBOOK

Answer these questions based on the situation described above.

1. List three ways that Emilio can learn more about how to perform the responsibilities listed on his job description form.

_____

_____

_____

2. Which of the following questions could Emilio answer using information from his job description form? Check all that apply.

_____ **a.** Will I be required to wear a uniform at work?

_____ **b.** What time do I get off work?

_____ **c.** What procedures are used to keep the laundry room clean?

_____ **d.** What personal qualities are important to my supervisor?

_____ **e.** Will I be required to pick up clothes from the residents?

_____ **f.** If there is a problem, whom should I report it to?

3. At the end of the first week, Emilio's supervisor compliments him on how quickly he is learning the job. Then she asks him to do a more thorough job of cleaning the laundry room floor before he ends his shift. Emilio feels angry about the criticism. He hasn't been mopping the floor every day because he thinks he is being asked to work harder than the other workers. Emilio should

(1) complain to his supervisor about the other workers

(2) accept the criticism and mop the floor well every day

(3) point out that cleaning the floor is not really his responsibility

(4) explain politely why the dirty floor isn't only his fault

Feedback

- If you got all of the answers right . . .   you have a foundation for learning workplace procedures and gaining new skills. Think about what you can do in the first few weeks on the job to better understand your employer's expectations.

- If you missed question 1 . . .   you need to explore different approaches to learning a new job.

- If you missed question 2 . . .   you need to think more about how you can use information from your employer to take responsibility for your own training.

- If you missed question 3 . . .   you need to think about how you can best use feedback from others to improve your performance on the job.

Vocabulary for *Learning at Work*

allowances	numbers that the government uses to figure out how much income tax should be withheld from an employee's paycheck during each pay period
assessments	checks or tests that measure how well an employee has accomplished a goal or is performing a task up to a certain standard
formal training	classroom instruction given to employees to provide information or teach a skill
job description	a document that explains the duties, responsibilities, and requirements for a particular job title
mandatory	required
payroll deductions	money that is withheld from an employee's paycheck
prioritize	to decide the order in which to do work tasks, based on their importance or urgency
routine	actions that are done regularly

PBS LiteracyLink®

Now watch Program 8.

After you watch, work on:
- pages 141–154 in this workbook
- Internet activities at www.pbs.org/literacy

Learning at Work

On the following pages, you will learn more about the ideas discussed in the video program and have an opportunity to develop your skills.

Think About the Key Points from the Video Program

To explore ways to learn a new job, you need to:
- Find out the extent of the training you will be given.
- Identify other ways to learn on the job.
- Be prepared to ask questions and manage the information you are given in response.

To meet your responsibility to take charge of your own training and prepare yourself to do the work:
- Complete required reading and fill out needed paperwork carefully.
- Learn to tell the difference between information you need now and information that can be learned over time.
- Use strategies to help you learn tasks more quickly.

Ongoing training can help you accomplish career goals and advance in your job. To take advantage of this opportunity:
- Take regular **assessments** of what you have learned and what you need to learn.
- Use job reviews to improve your performance on the job.
- Make a personal plan for learning more.

WORKTIP

As you begin a new job:
- Always respond well to suggestions and criticism from your employer and co-workers.
- Follow the company rules.
- Put in a full day's work.
- Ask questions if you do not understand an assignment.
- Be flexible and willing to change the way you have learned to do a task in the past.

Learning on the Job

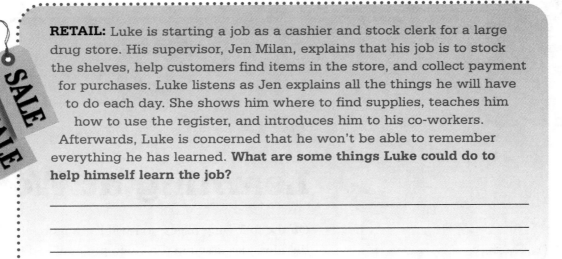

RETAIL: Luke is starting a job as a cashier and stock clerk for a large drug store. His supervisor, Jen Milan, explains that his job is to stock the shelves, help customers find items in the store, and collect payment for purchases. Luke listens as Jen explains all the things he will have to do each day. She shows him where to find supplies, teaches him how to use the register, and introduces him to his co-workers. Afterwards, Luke is concerned that he won't be able to remember everything he has learned. **What are some things Luke could do to help himself learn the job?**

_____

_____

_____

The first few weeks and months on a job are important to your success in that job. During that time, you will be trained to handle tasks that are new to you. You will also learn your new company's procedures for performing tasks that are familiar to you. Your responsibility during the training period is to use all the resources available to become a productive worker.

Learn from Company Training Programs

Some of the training you receive may be formal. **Formal training** has specific goals and methods of measuring your success. Formal training can be given in a class by an instructor or one on one with your supervisor.

Employers usually use formal training to teach safety procedures and to teach about the company's services or products. But they also may offer formal training to experienced employees who would like to move up in the company.

In a formal training situation, you will have to demonstrate that you understand the information either by taking a written test or by performing a task while the teacher observes you. You may receive a certificate that shows you have completed this part of your employee training.

Learn from Co-Workers

Your co-workers are an important resource for learning the job. Because your co-workers have actually done the work, they often know the best ways to approach a task. They have learned which procedures work well. They can also help you know what to do in a situation that isn't covered by normal procedures.

Learn by Example

One of the best ways to learn a new job is to watch co-workers and supervisors perform **routine** tasks.

By observing others, you can find out:
- What order in which to do a series of tasks
- What shortcuts may be helpful
- What materials are needed to complete the job
- How to keep a record of what has been done
- How to do a job safely
- How your job relates to other jobs in the workplace

Learn How Your Job Fits into the Big Picture

Learning a new job can be frustrating. At times, you may need more help than you are able to get. Remember that your training is just one of your supervisor's many duties. Be patient and try to see how your job fits into the entire workplace. Keep busy until you can get the information you need.

WORKTIP

To gain as much as possible from training:
- Use your time well. Always give the trainer your full attention.
- Take brief notes during the training session, and add to them immediately afterwards while the information is fresh in your mind.
- Soon after the training, practice the skills you have been taught.
- Control your emotions. It can be frustrating to learn new things, but you will catch on soon.

WorkSkills

1. On a separate piece of paper, list three ways to learn a new job.

2. During his first week on the job, Luke's supervisor shows him how to change the paper tape in his cash register. To make sure he understands the skill, Luke should

    (1) read the repair section of the register manual
    (2) ask his supervisor to demonstrate the task one more time
    (3) ask a co-worker to do it for him the first time he needs to change the paper
    (4) practice the skill as soon as possible

3. Luke has a chance to sign up for a formal class to learn more about the over-the-counter medicines the store sells. His co-worker tells him the classes are a big waste of time.

    _____

    _____

    _____

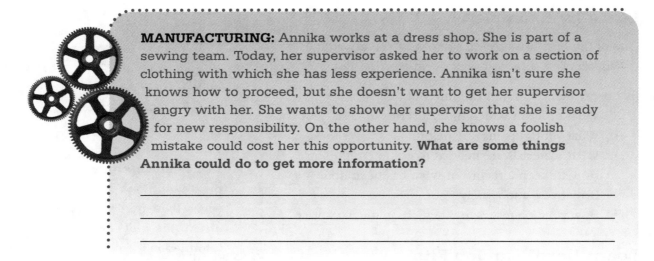

MANUFACTURING: Annika works at a dress shop. She is part of a sewing team. Today, her supervisor asked her to work on a section of clothing with which she has less experience. Annika isn't sure she knows how to proceed, but she doesn't want to get her supervisor angry with her. She wants to show her supervisor that she is ready for new responsibility. On the other hand, she knows a foolish mistake could cost her this opportunity. **What are some things Annika could do to get more information?**

_____

_____

_____

Learn from Print Information

Employers give workers a lot of information to read. They often rely on written messages to make sure all employees get the same information.

To learn best from print information, think about the purpose of the message. You may want to write a note on the top of the page to identify the subject. Underline important points. If the message asks you to take action in the future, make a note on your calendar to make sure that you follow through on time.

Organize the papers you receive from your employer. Carefully file and save information about work policies, employee benefits, and work procedures. You probably will need to refer to this information at a later date.

Learn by Asking Questions

One of the best ways to learn is to ask questions. Responsible workers make sure they have the information they need to do their jobs well. If you don't know what to do or how to do a job, asking questions may be the only way to find out. Don't try to cover up your lack of knowledge by pretending you know the answers.

Many times, you will be given directions on the job. To prevent mistakes, make notes of the steps to follow to complete a task. Then review your list and ask questions about any steps that may be unclear. Some workers make a small check next to any step or directions that they need more information about. Making a list is a good way to make sure you have all the information you need to do an important job.

You can check to make sure you have all the information you need by asking questions beginning with *who, what, when, where, why* or *how.* For example, suppose your supervisor is explaining how to order cleaning supplies. As you listen and take notes, you might think:

- Whom does this apply to?
- What am I being asked to do?
- When must this be done?
- Where do I turn in the order?
- Why does this concern me?

If the answers to these questions are not clear, you should ask the questions aloud. Your supervisor will appreciate that you are doing all you can to make sure you handle your job duties in a professional manner.

WorkSkills

1. During your shift, your supervisor hands you a form to fill out to sign up for dental insurance. You should

    (1) stop your work immediately and fill out the form
    (2) look at the form to find out when it is due
    (3) ask your supervisor whether you have to complete the form
    (4) put the form away until a day when you are not busy

2. In your own words, why is it important to ask questions if you don't understand something about your job?

    _____

    _____

TECH TIP

The Internet is a good source of information that can help you become a productive employee. You may be able to access the Internet at school or at a public library near your home.

The Internet has general information about what employers look for in their workers. It also has specific information about working in your career field. You can find tips on safety and getting along with co-workers. You can also find facts about your company and its competitors.

On a separate piece of paper, list at least five questions that you could use the Internet to answer. Underline key words in the sentences that you could use in an Internet search.

Taking Charge of Your Own Training

CONSTRUCTION: Kelli has just been hired as an assistant home inspector at Hooper Construction. On her first day on the job, she is given a W-4 form to fill out. She decides to claim only one allowance because the instructions don't make sense to her. When she gets her first check, she is surprised that so much money is taken out of her check for taxes. Kelli wonders if she should discuss the problem with her boss. She doesn't want him to think she isn't smart. **If you were Kelli, what would you do?**

_____

_____

_____

When you start a new job, there is much more to learn than how to perform your new job duties. You also need to learn your new company's rules and goals for its employees. You need to learn how your benefits work and make decisions about taxes and other **payroll deductions.**

Do Required Reading

Most information for employees is in written form. You probably will receive many handouts, booklets, and forms on the first few days of work. Make sure you read each piece of paper. To understand more when reading, first scan the paper for titles. Read each title or heading. Think about what kind of information the paper contains.

Then read the document. Look for words that tell you to take action, such as *mandatory* and *required.* These words are often followed by a due date or deadline. You may want to highlight these sentences with a marking pen. Make sure you act on these directions quickly.

Organize the information from your employer. You may need to refer to it later on. Set up a filing system using labels like these: Health Insurance, Use of Equipment, Safety Facts, Company Rules.

Your employer expects you to manage your own learning. When you receive written information, review it to see whether it is something you need to know right away. If it is, read it immediately. If not, set a goal for when you will have acquired the knowledge. Write the target date on the top of the paper. When you have a few minutes at work or at home, read a page from your file, and add it to your information filing system.

Complete All Forms

You will be asked to fill out many forms for health benefits and tax purposes. To make filling out forms easier, always read all directions before you start. Write neatly, and complete the forms to the best of your ability.

If you do not understand some items, ask your supervisor for help. If you work for a large company, you may be able to go to the personnel office for help.

You may have to talk to your spouse or family members to fill out some forms. For example, if you are married and covered by your spouse's health insurance, you may not want to sign up for health coverage through your employer. Accurately filling out health benefits forms is important. Usually, you can make changes to these forms only once a year.

Tax forms are affected by family earnings and your marital status. A W-4 form tells your employer how much federal income tax to withhold from your check. Using tables printed in the instructions, you choose a number of **allowances** to claim. You can turn in a new W-4 form at any time and change the number of allowances if your family's circumstances change.

> ### WORKTIP
>
> When you are asked to fill out any form:
> - Read the directions completely before you start.
> - Always use black ink.
> - Make a photocopy of completed forms for your own records.
> - Write something in every blank unless you are told otherwise.
> - Make sure you turn the form in on time to the correct person or department.

WorkSkills

Write *True* if the statement is true; *False* if it is false.

_____ 1. Forms that are mandatory can be filled out at your convenience.

_____ 2. You can submit new tax forms if your situation changes.

_____ 3. If you do not understand a question, you should leave it blank.

4. Why is it a good idea to keep all information from your employer on file?

_____

_____

5. What are some ways you can manage your own learning?

_____

_____

_____

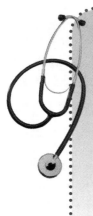

HEALTH CARE: Carma has been working as a filing clerk for a large health clinic for two weeks. Her supervisor, Jill Mesa, is very busy and hasn't spent much time with her. Carma has learned her job by watching the other workers. Several times today, Carma came across forms that she didn't know how to file. Because she doesn't want to bother Jill, she moved the forms to the bottom of the stack. She hopes she will know what to do by the time the forms come up again. **What do you think of Carma's decision? What could she do to take more responsibility for her own training?**

_____

_____

Prioritize Your Learning

Your employer understands that learning a new job is a process. It is not something you can do in one day, one week, or one month.

As your duties are explained to you, try to tell the difference between information you need to know right now and information that you can learn over time. Duties that you must carry out daily have top priority. You must learn these regular tasks quickly. Once you are doing well at your daily tasks, your supervisor will give you additional responsibilities. To advance in a company, you must be ready and willing to learn and accept new responsibilities.

Your **job description** can help you decide where to focus your energy. As you read through your job description, put a star by your regular responsibilities. During your training, pay close attention to information that relates to those duties.

Ask your supervisor for help in establishing priorities. Your supervisor will appreciate that you are concerned about making the most of your training.

Use Strategies to Improve Your Learning

You progress more quickly if you adopt these strategies to enhance your learning:

Repeat Key Information: To make sure you understand what your employer is trying to communicate, repeat the key points of the conversation aloud. Put the ideas in your own words. This gives your employer a chance to correct and add to the information you were given. Repeating key information helps prevent misunderstandings.

Make Notes About Key Steps: Keep a record of the information you are learning. Use a special notebook to write down policies and procedures that you must follow when doing your job.

Practice What You Have Learned: Soon after a task has been demonstrated or explained, try it for yourself. If possible, try the task while your supervisor is watching. As you practice, you will find out which parts of the task are unclear to you. Then you can ask for help and try again.

Ask for Feedback: Don't be afraid of criticism. Constructive criticism can help you make positive changes. If your supervisor or co-workers seem reluctant to give you feedback, ask for it. Make sure your work meets the standards set by your employer. Your employer will appreciate that you care about the needs of the company.

WorkSkills

1. According to the reading, you should first focus your energy on learning

    (1) those duties that will help you get promoted
    (2) facts about the company's products and services
    (3) the tasks that you must do every day
    (4) the key steps for all the tasks on your job description

2. In your own words, why is it important to seek feedback from your employer?

    _____

    _____

WRITE IT

You will be asked to fill out many forms on the job. Some forms relate to your hiring. Others are part of the work you do. Since most forms have certain things in common, it is a good idea to practice on your own.

Gather two forms for practice. Look for order forms in catalogs and magazines. Use credit application forms you get in the mail. Gather old health insurance forms or school applications.

Fill out the forms. Print neatly, using black ink. Think about your answer before you write it in the blank. Then ask a friend to look at your form and give feedback.

Training over the Long Term

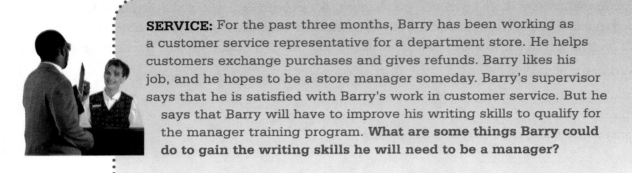

SERVICE: For the past three months, Barry has been working as a customer service representative for a department store. He helps customers exchange purchases and gives refunds. Barry likes his job, and he hopes to be a store manager someday. Barry's supervisor says that he is satisfied with Barry's work in customer service. But he says that Barry will have to improve his writing skills to qualify for the manager training program. **What are some things Barry could do to gain the writing skills he will need to be a manager?**

_____

_____

_____

As a worker, your learning process never ends. With each advancement in your career path, you will have new challenges and opportunities to learn.

Assess What You Have Learned

Successful workers continue to assess their skills and strengths long after they have found a job. Your skills and strengths are the key to success in your career path. By regularly assessing how you are doing, you can focus your energy on acquiring the skills you lack. You will also be prepared to take advantage of opportunities to advance your career.

Assessing your work requires thought and honesty. During the first few weeks, take stock often of what you have learned. You may want to keep a copy of your job description handy so that you can check off the duties that you have mastered.

For those duties that you have not learned completely, make a list of information that you need. Include any training that you need. Then, prioritize the items on the list. You may want to use check marks or stars to indicate items of importance. For instance, you could put two stars by items that you must learn as soon as possible, one star by those that can wait a little while, and no stars by those that have no immediate urgency.

After you have prioritized your learning needs, think about the top two or three items on the list. Decide what you can do to learn what you need to know. Some possibilities are reading company manuals, asking a supervisor for help, and asking a co-worker to demonstrate the task. You can also learn by observing others as they do their jobs.

Use Job Reviews to Set Goals

After you have been on the job a short period of time, you may be given a job review or evaluation. Your supervisor will meet with you to give positive feedback as well as discuss the areas in which you need improvement.

For most job reviews, your supervisor will rate you on work attitudes, personal qualities, and skills. Supervisors rarely give all high marks. Your job review is a chance for you to set goals to make improvements.

Try not to become defensive during a job review. Take responsibility for each area and think about ways to do better. If you are not sure how to make improvements, ask your supervisor for suggestions. Welcome any opportunities for additional training and guidance. Stay focused on the goal of learning how to do your job well.

WORKTIP

To find out more about moving up in your job:

- Read your employee handbook.
- Talk to your supervisor about how you can improve the quality of your work.
- Find out what skills and strengths you need to move to the next level.
- Set personal goals to acquire those skills and strengths.
- Ask for guidance during your next job review.

WorkSkills

Write *True* if the statement is true; *False* if it is false.

_____ 1. Employees are usually given a job review only if the supervisor is unhappy with their work.

_____ 2. The main purpose of a job review is to help you set goals to improve attitudes, personal qualities, and skills.

_____ 3. You should expect to be given some suggestions for improvement during your first job review.

4. During a job review, Barry's supervisor tells him that he needs to work on being friendly with all customers, even the difficult ones. Barry knows his supervisor is referring to a time last week when he was rude to a customer. Barry's best course of action would be to

(1) explain to his supervisor that the customer was rude first
(2) explain that the problem was caused by a co-worker
(3) set a goal to be friendly and professional with all customers
(4) set a goal to find a different job where he will be treated fairly

5. On a separate piece of paper, explain why is it important to assess your own job performance.

SERVICE: Mitch works for the maintenance department at a community college. He does small repair jobs like replacing broken panes of glass, changing locks, and replacing broken lighting fixtures. The college is offering all its employees a chance to take a computer class in the evening for no charge. Mitch has always been a little afraid of computers. Besides, he doesn't need a computer to do his work. Mitch thinks the class would be a waste of time. **Do you think Mitch should go to the class? Why?**

_____

_____

_____

Make a Personal Plan to Learn More

Think for a minute about your career path. Imagine yourself in the ideal job. What skills, experience, and knowledge will you need to succeed in that job? How will you gain these things?

Going to school can increase your knowledge and improve your skills, but it can never replace the insights you will gain by working. Each job you hold will give you new work experiences and the opportunity to improve your skills and learn new ones.

Once you recognize that the workplace is a place to learn, you are ready to develop a plan for success. Begin by making a list of skills that you expect to have before leaving the job you have now. Each skill becomes a learning goal. Keep the list in a place where you will see it often. As you work, look for chances to learn and practice the skills on your list.

Update Your Resume As You Learn

Eventually you will be ready to apply for a higher-level position within the company or look for a new job. In either case, you will need to submit an updated resume.

Don't wait until you need a resume to write one. Instead, update your old resume each time you learn a new skill, take on more responsibility, or change job titles. List professional courses and training that you receive at work. You can also list machines and computer software that you have learned to use. If you wait until later to add these facts to your resume, you may forget important details.

Now when you need to prepare the finished product, you will have all the facts you need at your fingertips to type a new resume.

Seek New Responsibilities

One way to gain new skills is to take on additional responsibilities. Projects that are outside your usual routine hold many opportunities for learning. Besides gaining new work skills, you can learn how to work well as part of a team. Some assignments offer opportunities to get to know employees and supervisors from other departments in the company. As you work with others, you continue to expand the base of your professional network.

You can also take on new responsibilities within your job. Once you have mastered your regular duties, your supervisor may ask you to add new ones. Instead of complaining that you are being asked to do more than everyone else, welcome these new duties as a chance to learn. Keep in mind that your hard work may soon be rewarded.

WorkSkills

1. Helene is happy with her job in manufacturing. Recently, her boss sent her to a training class to learn management skills. Why should she update her resume now if she doesn't plan to change jobs?

    _____

    _____

2. You have been asked to serve on the safety committee at work. How could taking on the extra responsibility help you in your career? List two possible benefits of serving on the committee.

    _____

    _____

    _____

WRITE IT

Writing a plan focuses your mind on your goals. You are more likely to accomplish your goals if you write them down.

Write a one-year learning plan. Use these steps:
* Choose three to five skills you would like to acquire during the coming year. They may be related to your work or personal life.
* Write one or two things you can do to learn and practice each skill.
* Write a date by which you plan to have learned each skill.
* Post your plan where you will see it often.

Review

RETAIL: Sandy is starting a new job at Park's Electronics, a store that specializes in computers, stereo equipment, and other electronic devices. The store also offers computer classes in the evening for its customers. Store employees can sign up for the classes for a small fee.

Sandy will be working in the computer department. Her main responsibility will be selling software programs.

Sandy is expected to keep up to date about changes in computer technology. Her boss tells her to make sure that the products the customers choose will meet their needs. Whenever possible, the store wants to avoid returns of merchandise.

1. Sandy knows a lot about computers, but after three days on the job, she is frustrated. She still hasn't made a sale. Instead, she notices that most customers go to one of her co-workers before they make a final decision. She realizes that she needs to learn more about how to sell products. List three ways she could learn more about selling.

    _____

    _____

    _____

2. Sandy's supervisor, Eliza Kang, schedules a time to meet with her to explain the store's products and policies. To get the most out of her training, what three strategies can Sandy use to improve her learning?

    _____

    _____

    _____

3. At a staff meeting, Sandy's supervisor announces that the company is offering a training course about a new computer system that the company is selling. Even though Sandy does not sell computer systems, she could benefit by taking the course. List two ways the course could help her career.

    _____

    _____

    _____

    _____

Skills Review

Questions 1–4 are based on the following situation.

SERVICE: Dasha is learning more about careers in business. She would like to work in an office. Dasha enjoys using a computer and can type 45 words per minute. She wants to improve her computer skills.

Dasha needs to find a job soon. To support her daughter and herself, she needs to earn at least $1,475 per month. One of her friends, Carla, who does word processing for an insurance company, earns $1,900 a month. Dasha hopes to start out as a data entry keyer and work her way up to a better paying job. Besides earning money, Dasha needs to find a job with daytime hours and good health benefits.

1. Dasha's cousin tells her about a data entry job in the records office at the high school. What are some things Dasha needs to find out to see whether the job at the school will meet her needs? Check all that apply.

    _____ **a.** the health benefits offered
    _____ **b.** the monthly salary for the job
    _____ **c.** hours of the job, part-time or full-time
    _____ **d.** the job's daily schedule

2. Dasha finds out that the job pays $1,425 a month. It has good health benefits and daytime hours. She can qualify for an additional $80 per month if she passes a computer course offered by the school district. The course is free to all school employees. If supporting her family and improving her skills are Dasha's top priorities, she should

    (1) take the job and sign up for the computer course soon
    (2) look for a job in word processing
    (3) go back to school full-time
    (4) look for a job with more opportunities for advancement

3. Dasha has an information interview with Carla's boss, Wilbur Todd. What should Dasha do to make the meeting a success? Check all that apply.

    _____ **a.** wear clothes that are appropriate for working in an office
    _____ **b.** bring a notebook to take notes during the interview
    _____ **c.** plan to take about an hour of Wilbur Todd's time
    _____ **d.** prepare several questions to ask during the interview

4. Besides talking to family, friends, and neighbors, what are two other sources of information Dasha can use to find out more about working in an office? Write your answer on a separate piece of paper.

Questions 5–7 are based on the following situation.

HEALTH CARE: Daniel is interested in a job in health care. He is taking classes in the evening to become a medical assistant. He hopes someday to become a Physician Assistant. To help pay for his schooling, Daniel is looking for a daytime job related to his career field.

Daniel doesn't have any work experience in the health field, but he did help care for his elderly grandfather last year. He has also volunteered at a nursing home in his neighborhood. Both his instructor and the director at the nursing home have agreed to be references for him.

Daniel is looking for job leads by reading the want ads every day. He also visits the public career counseling service to read the job postings. On Friday he found the following newspaper advertisement:

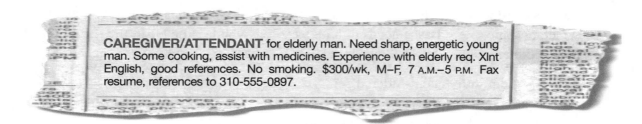

CAREGIVER/ATTENDANT for elderly man. Need sharp, energetic young man. Some cooking, assist with medicines. Experience with elderly req. Xlnt English, good references. No smoking. $300/wk, M–F, 7 A.M.–5 P.M. Fax resume, references to 310-555-0897.

5. Which of these is a true statement about Daniel's skills and qualifications for this job?

   (1) Daniel does not have the necessary skills to apply for the job.
   (2) Daniel needs to take special classes to learn how to care for the elderly.
   (3) Many of the skills that Daniel acquired in his volunteer work can be transferred to this job as a caretaker.
   (4) The employer will not be interested in Daniel's experience with his grandfather.

6. How could this job help Daniel in his career? Check all that apply.

   _____ **a.** He will have plenty of time to study for his classes.
   _____ **b.** He can gain work experience that will qualify him for other jobs.
   _____ **c.** He may make professional contacts in the medical field.
   _____ **d.** He can earn the money he needs to take additional classes.

7. Daniel found the job listed under the key word Caregiver. When searching for job leads, why is it a good idea to read the entire want ads section?

   (1) The want ads are organized alphabetically.
   (2) Employers may list jobs using an uncommon key word.
   (3) You can find out what key word sections have the most jobs.
   (4) The employer may have listed the job in the wrong section.

Questions 8–12 are based on the following situation.

RETAIL: Eunsook heard from her neighbor about a job opening as a cashier at DK Clothing. Eunsook has never worked in a store, but she did work as a cashier at a school cafeteria. She has experience handling cash, making change, and running an electronic cash register.

Eunsook is very interested in the job at the clothing store. She would like to learn more about retail sales and take classes in management. She visited the store the next day to find out how to apply. Eli Graham, the store manager, gave her a job application form to take home and fill out.

Write *True* if the statement is true; *False* if it is false.

_____ 8. The job application form asks for the dates of employment for Eunsook's last job. If she doesn't know these dates, she could leave the spaces blank.

_____ 9. If Eunsook has already prepared a resume, she could give her resume, instead of the job application form, to the employer.

10. Eli may screen out Eunsook's job application form for any of the following reasons. Check all that apply.

_____ **a.** messy handwriting
_____ **b.** incomplete answers
_____ **c.** writing N/A if an answer is not applicable
_____ **d.** not signing and dating the form
_____ **e.** giving untruthful information

11. Eunsook's job at the school lasted only three months. She was filling in for an employee on a leave of absence. When the temporary job ended, the school offered her a full-time position, but she turned it down because she didn't like the person who would be supervising her. What should Eunsook write in the space marked "Reason for Leaving Job"?

(1) "I did not want a full-time job."
(2) "My supervisor was hard to work with."
(3) "The job was temporary."
(4) Eunsook should not list the job at the cafeteria on the form.

12. Near the end of the application form, Eunsook is asked, "Why do you want to work for DK Clothing?" In her answer, Eunsook should

(1) write about her skills, strengths, and career goals
(2) tell a little about her family and background
(3) explain in detail why the job at the cafeteria didn't work out
(4) write about her personal circumstances and financial needs

Questions 13–18 are based on the following situation.

RETAIL: Kyle is applying for a job as an order clerk for an automotive parts store. The job as an order clerk is full-time. It pays $10 per hour. Because the store is small, there are not many chances to move up in the company. Kyle will not need any special training. His supervisor will teach him everything that he needs to know.

Kyle needs to find a job very soon. He needs to earn at least $9.50 per hour to pay his bills. Moving up in the company is important to Kyle, but paying his bills is his number one priority.

13. To apply for the job, Kyle will need to turn in a resume. The work experience section of the resume should include

    (1) a list of his work skills, including any computer experience
    (2) a paragraph explaining what kind of job Kyle is looking for
    (3) the date Kyle graduated from high school
    (4) facts about the jobs Kyle has had in the past

Read these statements about how employers use resumes as part of the application process. Write *True* if the statement is true; *False* if it is false.

_____ 14. An employer may call your previous supervisors to verify the dates you have listed on your resume.

_____ 15. Your resume should include your age, height, and weight.

_____ 16. An employer assumes your resume is a sample of your best work.

17. Besides the job at the automotive parts store, Kyle is also considering a job with a large furniture store. The job pays $9 per hour, but he could be promoted after working there for a year. Based on what you know of Kyle's priorities, Kyle should

    (1) take the job at the automotive store
    (2) take the job at the furniture store
    (3) go back to school so that he can qualify for a better job
    (4) keep looking until he finds a job that offers both good pay and advancement opportunities

18. Kyle decides to list the pros and cons of both jobs to help him reach a decision. Which of the following could Kyle list in the pro column for the job at the furniture store?

    (1) high salary
    (2) on-the-job training
    (3) opportunities for advancement
    (4) small company

Questions 19–24 are based on the following situation.

SERVICE: Rhonda has a job interview with Lucy Lai at Westside Recycling. The recycling company processes the aluminum cans, glass, and paper collected by the city's recycling program.

Rhonda is a hard worker. In a previous job, she worked at Al's Market, a small grocery store, to unpack deliveries and stock shelves. On the job, she demonstrated that she is reliable and honest. Her boss at the grocery store has written a letter recommending her for the new job.

19. To begin the interview, Lucy says, "Tell me about your job at Al's Market." Rhonda can best answer the question by talking about

    (1) the reasons why she enjoyed working at a grocery store
    (2) her strengths, skills, and work attitudes
    (3) some of the problems at the market
    (4) the reason why she left the job

20. Rhonda previously worked for three months as a helper at a construction site. Lucy asks Rhonda her reason for leaving the job so soon. Actually, Rhonda left the job because her supervisor treated her unfairly. Rhonda felt the supervisor didn't want a woman working on his crew. Rhonda quit when she found the better-paying job at the market. To answer the interview question, Rhonda should

    (1) explain that the construction work was very tiring and that she needed a less demanding job
    (2) complain about her supervisor's unfair treatment of her
    (3) explain that she was better suited for the grocery store job
    (4) tell Lucy that the job ended and her employer let her go

Write *True* if the statement is true; *False* if it is false.

_____ 21. It is legal for an employer to choose not to hire you if you are not physically able to do the job.

_____ 22. Eye contact and good posture can suggest that you are confident and honest.

_____ 23. An employer must hire the applicant with the best skills.

24. Before she leaves the interview, Rhonda should ask

    (1) "How many days of sick leave do I get each month?"
    (2) "Could you explain the health benefits that come with the job?"
    (3) "When will you be making a decision?"
    (4) "How long would I need to work here to earn vacation pay?"

Questions 25–28 are based on the following situation.

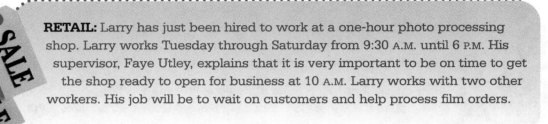

RETAIL: Larry has just been hired to work at a one-hour photo processing shop. Larry works Tuesday through Saturday from 9:30 A.M. until 6 P.M. His supervisor, Faye Utley, explains that it is very important to be on time to get the shop ready to open for business at 10 A.M. Larry works with two other workers. His job will be to wait on customers and help process film orders.

25. On his first day, Larry feels uncomfortable because he doesn't know what to do with his time. The store isn't busy and his supervisor called in sick. The other workers tell him he can go home early if he wants to. Larry should

    (1) stay at work and do the best he can to learn more about the job
    (2) run some errands; then check back to see if they need him at the store
    (3) complain to his co-workers about how poorly the store is managed
    (4) leave for the day and plan to put in a full day tomorrow

26. The next day the store is busier. Larry is assigned to take his half hour lunch break at 12:30. He would rather go at 1 o'clock so that he can have lunch with a friend. Larry should

    (1) try to talk a co-worker into changing lunch times with him
    (2) leave a little late for lunch and come back at 1:30
    (3) ask Faye for permission to take a long lunch
    (4) go to lunch from 12:30 to 1:00

27. What do most employers expect of new employees? Check all that apply.

    _____ **a.** put in a full day's work
    _____ **b.** avoid all mistakes
    _____ **c.** use their time well
    _____ **d.** do the work without asking a lot of questions
    _____ **e.** know the job by the end of the first day
    _____ **f.** treat co-workers with respect

28. At the end of the second day, Larry accidentally put a customer's photographs in the wrong envelope. When the customer came to pick up his film, no one could find the photographs. The customer was upset. When Faye told him to be more careful, Larry felt angry. Larry should

    (1) tell Faye that he is upset with her treatment of him
    (2) pay more attention to the details of his job
    (3) look for a job where he is treated better
    (4) pretend the mistake wasn't his fault

Questions 29–34 are based on the following situation.

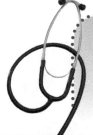

HEALTH CARE: Naima works in the records office of a busy health clinic. She files patient records and prepares some files for microfilming. Naima's job involves some lifting and moving of boxes of records. The following safety guidelines are posted on the wall in the workroom.

PREVENT BACK INJURIES — ALWAYS LIFT SAFELY

- When lifting, keep your back straight, bend your knees, and keep your feet apart. Use your legs for lifting as much as possible.

- Tighten your stomach muscles as you lift. Do not hold your breath.

- Keep the item close to your body.

- To move to the side, pivot and turn instead of twisting your back.

- Use a hand truck or cart to move boxes more than a few feet.

---

29. Naima's office recently purchased a new aluminum hand truck with a locking brake. Naima isn't sure how to use the brake. What should she do? Check all that apply.

 _____ **a.** Use the new hand truck to move boxes without setting the brake.

 _____ **b.** Ask a co-worker to demonstrate how to use the equipment.

 _____ **c.** Read the instruction manual that came with the hand truck.

 _____ **d.** Practice setting the brake on the hand truck without a heavy load.

30. Naima needs to move a heavy box of records from a high shelf. She isn't sure she can move the box by herself. Naima's employer will expect her to

 (1) use her lower back to lift the box
 (2) hold her breath as she moves the box
 (3) twist her back to move the box to the side
 (4) ask a co-worker for help

Write *True* if the statement is true; *False* if it is false.

 _____ 31. Naima needs to apply the safety guidelines only when lifting packages that are too heavy for her.

 _____ 32. Many accidents occur when workers feel tired or rushed.

 _____ 33. If an accident happens, you should report it at once even if no one was seriously injured.

34. One of Naima's co-workers tripped on a power cord stretched across a walkway. Naima should

 (1) be careful each time she walks by the cord
 (2) tell her supervisor that the cord may be a hazard
 (3) put up a sign warning her co-workers to be careful
 (4) remove the hazard by unplugging the cord

Questions 35–40 are based on the following situation.

RETAIL: Tim was just hired as a cashier at a small restaurant. To help him learn the job, the owner gives him an employee handbook and a booklet on health regulations. Ann, the manager of the day shift, is assigned to train him.

Ann first teaches Tim how to work the register. Then she shows him how to process credit card payments. Tim is required to ask the customer for a picture identification card, compare the signature on the identification card to the one on the credit card, and check the credit card's expiration date. Then he can accept the card as payment.

35. A customer wants to pay with a credit card. The customer claims he left his driver's license at home. Tim hasn't been taught what to do in this situation. Ann is on a break and other customers are waiting. Tim should

    (1) ask a co-worker for help
    (2) explain to the customer that he is a new hire and ask him to pay some other way
    (3) look up the problem in the employee handbook
    (4) accept the credit card as payment

36. Tim would like to learn more about working in restaurant management. What are some things that Tim can do to take responsibility for gaining new skills? Check all that apply.

    _____ **a.** Ask Ann to teach him her job.
    _____ **b.** Offer to take on extra responsibilities.
    _____ **c.** Give suggestions to co-workers for better ways to do their jobs.
    _____ **d.** Observe Ann doing her job.
    _____ **e.** Read the employee handbook.

Write *True* if the statement is true; *False* if it is false.

    _____ 37. To learn a new job, focus first on the routine tasks.
    _____ 38. A job review is a chance for you to give your supervisor
               suggestions on how to do his or her job better.
    _____ 39. Employers expect new workers to ask very few questions.

40. At the end of the first week, Ann tells Tim that he needs to be a little more friendly when he greets the customers. Tim feels defensive. He thinks Ann may be trying to push him to quit. Tim should

    (1) complain to his co-workers about how Ann is treating him
    (2) use the suggestion to help improve his performance
    (3) explain that he may have been tired the day she observed him
    (4) accuse Ann of looking for any excuse to get rid of him

Skills Review Answer Key

1. a, b, c

2. (1) take the job and sign up for the computer course soon

3. a, b, d

4. Any two of the following: information interviews; a career counseling service; the library; the Internet; people she meets; community, technical, and vocational colleges

5. (3) Many of the skills that Daniel acquired in his volunteer work can be transferred to this job as a caretaker.

6. b, c, d

7. (2) Employers may list jobs using an uncommon key word.

8. False

9. False

10. a, b, d, e

11. (3) "The job was temporary."

12. (1) write about her skills, strengths, and career goals

13. (4) facts about the jobs Kyle has had in the past

14. True

15. False

16. True

17. (1) take the job at the automotive store

18. (3) opportunities for advancement

19. (2) her strengths, skills, and work attitudes

20. (3) explain that she was better suited for the grocery store job

21. True

22. True

23. False

24. (3) "When will you be making a decision?"

25. (1) stay at work and do the best he can to learn more about the job

26. (4) go to lunch from 12:30 to 1:00

27. a, c, f

28. (2) pay more attention to the details of his job

29. b, c, d

30. (4) ask a co-worker for help

31. False

32. True

33. True

34. (2) tell her supervisor that the cord may be a hazard

35. (1) ask a co-worker for help

36. b, d, e

37. True

38. False

39. False

40. (2) use the suggestion to help improve his performance

Skills Review Evaluation Chart

Circle the question numbers that you answered correctly. Then fill in the number of questions you got correct for each program lesson. Find the total number correct, and review the lessons you had trouble with.

Program Lesson	Question Number	Number Correct/Total
1: *Planning to Work* Thinking About Work, Making a Career Plan, Researching Jobs and Careers	1, 2, 3, 4	____/4
2: *Matching Skills and Jobs* Assessing Your Employability, Finding Job Leads, Making the Job Search Your Job	5, 6, 7	____/3
3: *Applying for Jobs* Figuring Out the Application Process, Learning How Employers Screen Job Seekers, Completing Job Application Forms	8, 9, 10, 11, 12	____/5
4: *Resumes, Tests, and Choices* Understanding the Purposes of Resumes, Deciding Which Job Openings to Pursue, Comparing Job Opportunities	13, 14, 15, 16, 17, 18	____/6
5: *Interviewing* Exploring the Interview Process, Preparing for an Interview, Interviewing and Follow-Up	19, 20, 21, 22, 23, 24	____/6
6: *Ready for Work* Understanding Your Employer's Expectations, Learning the Meaning of "Work-Ready," Working as a New Hire	25, 26, 27, 28	____/4
7: *Workplace Safety* Understanding Safety Issues, Recognizing Safety Issues, Learning How to Protect Yourself and Your Co-workers	29, 30, 31, 32, 33, 34	____/6
8: *Learning at Work* Learning on the Job, Taking Charge of Your Own Training, Training over the Long Term	35, 36, 37, 38, 39, 40	____/6
	Total	____/40

WHAT YOUR SCORE MEANS

If you got 36–40 correct: You are ready to work. You have a good understanding of how to find job leads, represent your skills and strengths, and communicate well with co-workers, supervisors, and employees.

If you got 32–35 correct: You understand how to find job leads and manage your own learning on the job. Review the sections for the items you missed to improve your chances of succeeding on the job.

If you got 28–31 correct: You need to improve your understanding of the employment process and your relationship to it. Review any program in which you missed more than one item.

If you got fewer than 28 correct: You need to review the basic principles in each program. As you read, think about what employers are looking for in a job applicant. Think about how to take responsibility for your own learning on the job. By reviewing the programs and doing the exercises in this book, you can gain the knowledge and skills you need.

Answer Key

PROGRAM 1: PLANNING TO WORK

Thinking About Work

WorkSkills, page 17

1. a, b, c, e, g

2. Bonita needs to know the total of her fixed expenses. This is the basic amount of money she needs to earn. She will also probably want to estimate how much she needs for things not included in fixed expenses, such as travel and entertainment. She should also think about saving a little each month.

WorkSkills, page 19

1. Any two of the following: To find job satisfaction, to take pride in my accomplishments, to find and overcome challenges, and to contribute to the community

2. Any two of the following: Being friendly to all customers no matter how you feel, handling complaints, and getting along with co-workers and supervisors

3. (3)

Write It, page 19

You should have five services or products listed. For each item on your list, you should have a list of jobs or kinds of businesses that help produce the product or service or make it available.

Making a Career Plan

WorkSkills, page 21

1. Any four of the following: Friends, family, neighbors, people in the community, the public library, books, magazines, newspapers, and the Internet

2. Any three of the following: Manager, food servers, host or hostess, people who bus tables, cleaning crew, and bookkeeper

3. True

4. False

5. False

WorkSkills, page 23

1. a, c, d

2. False

3. True

4. False

5. Both grants and loans can be used to pay for the cost of education. Grants do not have to be paid back. Loans must be paid back, usually with interest.

Tech Tip, page 23

You should have listed five words or phrases that relate to your career area. Check to make sure each item is specific, not general. For example, if you wanted to find work as a gardener or landscaper, the specific phrase "working to maintain landscaping" would be better than the general phrase "outdoor work."

Researching Jobs and Careers

WorkSkills, page 25

1. a, c, e

2. (2)

WorkSkills, page 27

1. a, b, d, f

2. False

3. True

4. False

5. Setting goals is the key to staying on track. It should help Ron end up where he wants to be in his career. If Ron isn't sure what he wants to do with his life, he may end up in a job that is wrong for him. Then he may be unhappy with his job and want to quit.

Write It, page 27

Your paragraphs should summarize the information you have gathered about the job you would most like to have. Check to make sure you have included the title of the job, a description of its duties, and the training you would need to do the job.

Review, page 28

1. b, c, d, f, g

2. The sales job. This job promises a large salary, which Marilyn could begin earning immediately if she does the job well.

3. Any of the following: Conduct information interviews; use career counseling services; gather information from family, friends, and neighbors; do research at a public library; investigate using the Internet

PROGRAM 2:
MATCHING SKILLS AND JOBS

Assessing Your Employability
WorkSkills, page 35

1. a. A   e. T
   b. T   f. T
   c. T   g. A
   d. A   h. A

2. (2)

3. Any of the following: Doing research, analyzing information, meeting and dealing with new people, keeping records, asking good questions, being a good listener, speaking clearly, writing letters, using business machines, filling out forms, being patient

WorkSkills, page 37

1. b, d

2. Compare your answers to these samples:

   Adaptive skill: motivated

   Example: I stayed after school to get extra time in the school's computer lab so I could learn word processing.

   Transferable skill: teaching skills to others

   Example: I volunteered at the Children's Museum on Fridays to help elementary school children do art and science projects.

Write It, page 37

You should have defined and described a specific skill that you want to acquire and a list of steps to achieve your goal. You should have written a date of completion for each step and a date for your overall goal to be achieved.

Finding Job Leads
WorkSkills, page 39

1. a, b, c, e, g

2. While working at a job pumping gas, Omar can learn more about the kinds of problems motorists experience with their cars, trucks, and vans. If the station has an automotive department, Omar would have the opportunity to meet the mechanics and learn about their work. He can learn more about how to communicate with and serve the public.

3. Reasons may include the following: To learn the names of job titles, to find out how much the employers in your area pay for certain kinds of work, to learn about the job outlook for your career in your community, and to find job leads. You may have identified other reasons as well.

WorkSkills, page 41

1. (2)

2. (4)

3. Questions may include any of the following. You may have other questions as well.

   • What kinds of skills will I need to succeed in sales?

   • What is the best way to get started in retail sales?

   • What did you like best about working in sales?

   • What kinds of training could be helpful to me in order to advance in my career?

   • Do you know anyone else I could talk to in order to learn more about the clothing industry?

   • Which companies are best to work for, and why?

   • Which companies should I avoid, and why?

   • Do you know of any current openings?

Communicate, page 41

When your friend read each article, you should have listened for main ideas and details. Your goal is to improve your ability to listen and remember. Did it improve your recall to make a list of notes immediately after your friend finished reading? Did you write down only the most important points?

Making the Job Search Your Job
WorkSkills, page 43

1. a, b, d, f

2. Instructors, teachers, or school counselors; neighbors; other workers in your community; former employers and co-workers; librarians; people from church or some other organization to which you belong

3. Visit a career counseling service; visit businesses and talk to employers and workers; talk to family, friends, and neighbors; talk with other people in her network and expand her network

WorkSkills, page 45

1. DATA ENTRY Part-time worker needed now, Monday through Friday, 30 hours per week, some evenings, $8.90 per hour to start, keyboarding—40 or more words per minute required, 1 year minimum office experience preferred. Call Jeff at (213) 555-5490.

2. a, c, d, e, f

Read It, page 45

You should have found out which day's newspaper has the greatest number of want ads and obtained a newspaper for that day. Then you should have scanned the entire list of want ads, searching for jobs in your career field. For each job listing in your career, you should have noted the key word. You also should have kept a tally of how many advertisements were listed under each key word.

Review, page 46

1. Any three of the following: Kevin has transferable skills in music and arts, experience planning activities, as well as counseling and tutoring experience. He is also bilingual.

2. By reading the entire want ads section, Kevin may find jobs that he is qualified for that have been listed under a variety of headings, both common and uncommon.

3. Kevin could network by talking to his family and friends, instructors, and workers in the community. He could research companies in his area by using resources at the school library. He could visit a career counseling service to find local job leads. He could also use the Internet to look for job openings.

4. Questions may include the following:
   - What skills do I need to develop to find a job as a teacher's aide?
   - What is the best way to go about finding a job in education?
   - Can you suggest anyone else I should talk to about working as an educational aide?

   You may have other questions as well.

PROGRAM 3: APPLYING FOR JOBS

Figuring Out the Application Process

WorkSkills, page 53

1. (2)

2. (4)

3. Tasha should change from her workout clothes into conservative clothes that are neat and clean. If Tasha wears her workout clothes to drop off the application, the employer may think that she doesn't care about making a professional impression. The employer may assume she will be careless about her appearance on the job.

WorkSkills, page 55

1. b, c, e

2. Matt could make a photocopy of the form and practice fitting his answers in the spaces.

3. Matt could improve his answer by writing in complete sentences and writing only about a career in mining. "Building houses" is a change of subject and suggests that Matt has not really made up his mind about what he wants to do. Here is an example of how this could be rewritten: *I have been interested in mining and construction equipment all of my life. Someday, I would like to become an operating engineer for a mining company.*

Write It, page 55

Your worksheet should list your work, educational, and volunteer experiences, starting with the most recent experience. You should have filled in each blank for each experience listed.

Learning How Employers Screen Job Seekers

WorkSkills, page 57

1. (3)

2. A job application form is a sample of your work. If you do not follow the directions exactly, the employer may assume you are not good at following directions.

3. No, it is not a good idea. The employer may discover the lie during a background check. If you give false information on an application form, you may not be hired. If the employer discovers Gary's lie after he is hired, he may be fired.

WorkSkills, page 59

1. False
2. True
3. False
4. False
5. Your answer should include information about your skills and work attitude. Your answer may read something like this: *I am a hard worker who is highly motivated to learn. I have good communication skills. I enjoy meeting new people and helping others.*
6. Monica should emphasize her positive attitude, skills, and strengths. She should mention specifically how her experience reshelving or "filing" books according to their code will help the employer.

Write It, page 59

You should have written a cover letter, referring to Sample Cover Letter and How to Type a Business Letter. You should then have had an instructor or someone else read your cover letter. You should then have revised it based on feedback.

Math Matters, page 60

For the $7 per hour example:
$7 x 40 hours = $280, the weekly wage
$280 x 52 weeks = $14,560, the annual wage
$14,560 ÷ 12 months = $1,213.33, the monthly wage

WorkSkills, pages 61–63

To check your work, make sure you wrote something in every blank of the application form. You should have printed neatly using black ink. You may want to show your work to a friend or your instructor and ask for suggestions.

Review, page 64

Your answers should be similar to these:

1. Even though the two documents contain much of the same information, they have different purposes. The resume demonstrates Sharon's ability to write clearly and organize information. The job application form is designed by the company, which makes it easy for Ed to find the information he needs. Because all applicants fill out the same form, the employer can easily compare several applicants' answers.
2. Any of the following: Not following directions; giving false information; failing to include important, helpful information; leaving questions unanswered; volunteering negative information; leaving smudges; using poor handwriting; or not signing the application.

3. Sharon's special skills show that she has many talents and an aptitude for learning. Sharon could explain how she could use her special skills to help the company. She should emphasize her friendliness and enjoyment of meeting the public, both skills that would help her on the job. Her special skills also indicate that she is a well-rounded person with many interests. Even though these skills are not directly related to the job, they are examples of Sharon's many strengths.

PROGRAM 4: RESUMES, TESTS, AND CHOICES

Understanding the Purposes of Resumes

WorkSkills, page 71

1. Unlike a job application, a resume is designed and written by the job applicant. This allows the applicant to highlight the skills and experiences that are best suited to the job opening.
2. If your employer discovers that you lied about one thing on your resume, he or she may assume other information is false as well. The employer is not likely to hire you. If the employer discovers a lie on your resume after hiring you, you may be fired.
3. c, d

WorkSkills, page 73

1. Personal information such as a description of your appearance can be used to discriminate against you.
2. (3)
3. Any two of the following: Huong can recognize high-quality fabrics; follows the latest styles and trends; enjoys helping people shop for clothes for special occasions

Read It, page 73

You should have found at least ten descriptive words or phrases that you feel describe you. Examples may include *motivated, trustworthy, takes initiative, dependable, good communicator, hard-working, detail-oriented.*

Deciding Which Job Openings to Pursue

WorkSkills, page 75

1. (1)

2. (4)

3. You should have listed your two most important priorities in a new job and indicated which is the highest priority, or most important factor. You should also have explained why these factors are so important to you.

WorkSkills, page 77

1. Your answer should include the following information: After working at a job for a year, you would know the duties well and can do your best work. This can help impress your employer, who may give you opportunities for advancement, training to gain new skills, a pay raise, and other benefits. A stay of at least one year will make your employer more willing to give you a good recommendation. Also, it is likely to make a better impression on your next employer.

2. (3)

Communicate, page 77

You should have listed ten questions about the working conditions at the employee's workplace. For example, you may ask questions such as

- "What is the dress code?"
- "Are the hours flexible?"
- "Are employees treated with respect?"
- "Is the atmosphere friendly?"
- "Is there much overtime? Is it required?"
- "Is there much tension or conflict?"
- "Is it noisy or quiet?"
- "How much pressure is there?"
- "Are there opportunities to take breaks, especially for lunch?"
- "Are there opportunities for further training?"
- "Are there good opportunities for advancement?"

Comparing Job Opportunities

WorkSkills, page 79

1. Your answer should explain that listing the pros and cons can help you decide if a job is right for you and which job would be best for you.

2. (2)

3. (4)

WorkSkills, page 81

1. Any two of the following: he could ask an information officer at the bank or ask for an informational brochure about the bank; he could look for the information in the public library; he could conduct a search on the Internet.

2. False

3. False

4. False

5. True

Math Matters, page 81

Your paragraph should say whether your expected salary will cover the additional costs involved with the job you are considering. To reach your answer, you probably took the following steps:

- Add together the monthly costs involved with the new job. This total is your new costs.
- Add the new costs to the cost of your monthly basic needs. This is your total monthly spending.
- Subtract your total monthly spending from your expected monthly salary. Remember to use the expected net salary—the total salary minus taxes and other deductions—rather than the gross, or total salary.
- If an amount is left over, your salary should be enough to cover the costs of the new job. If nothing is left over, or if there is a negative amount, your salary is not enough to cover the new costs.

Review, page 82

1. Your entry should have the following information: Takes orders, serves food and beverages, prepares bills and accepts payments, seats customers, sets up and clears tables, works two shifts daily.

2. Yes, the job meets Kina's needs. It is a full-time job in the health field. The pay is $280 per week (assuming 40 hours per week as full-time at $7 per hour). For some weeks, Kina's current job might pay more depending on how good the tips are. The nurse's aide job offers on-the-job training and an opportunity to apply for health benefits after three months.

3. Listing the pros and cons and then evaluating them can help Kina decide if the job will fit her needs. By evaluating the pros and cons, Kina can determine if the positive factors outweigh the negative factors, or vice versa.

PROGRAM 5: INTERVIEWING

Exploring the Interview Process

WorkSkills, page 89

1. (3)

2. No, Paul's answer shows that he hasn't given much thought to his career plan. He volunteers the information that he may not be willing to make a long-term commitment to the job. The employer will probably not be interested in hiring him.

3. Julissa needs to answer the question "What did you like least about your last job?" Her answer could have been something like this: *My job was very demanding during rush times when the lines were long. Even though I had to work faster, I had to make sure that I gave each customer my full attention and practiced good listening skills to make sure I got the order right.* In this answer, the focus is on Julissa's skills and strengths, not on her complaints.

WorkSkills, page 91

1. (3)

2. False

3. True

4. True

Communicate, page 91

The purpose of this exercise is to find out how others see you. You should have asked three people who know you well to name your greatest strength. After making a list of the information they gave you, you should have thought about how this information can help you in a job interview.

Preparing for an Interview

WorkSkills, page 93

1. From Sherry's answer, you can see that she enjoys working, learning, helping people, and finding solutions to problems. She is also patient, thoughtful, and kind. You can also see that she is a good communicator because she thinks about what the employer needs and addresses his concerns.

2. Sherry enjoys work. She clearly thinks the customer is important and will treat people with respect. She welcomes challenges and shows a desire to learn and to accept more responsibility.

WorkSkills, page 95

1. If you plan your questions in advance, you will not have trouble thinking of a question on the spot. Employers expect you to want to know more about the job. If you don't ask anything, they may think you are not very interested in the job or are not well-prepared for the interview.

2. (1)

Communicate, page 95

You should have chosen three personal qualities in advance and then asked a friend to ask you two common interview questions. Your goal was to communicate the personal qualities through body language and attitude. After the interview, you should have shared the list of qualities with your friend and asked how well you communicated the qualities.

Interviewing and Follow-Up

WorkSkills, page 97

1. Making eye contact helps you communicate. You can interpret the interviewer's facial expressions and body language if you make frequent eye contact. Also, making eye contact shows confidence and honesty.

2. "No, I don't have a car yet, but I do have reliable transportation to work. You can count on me to be here on time every day."

3. (3)

WorkSkills, page 99

1. (4)

2. During the second interview, the employer will probably discuss salary, benefits, and the work schedule. Janelle may also have to take skills tests. Being asked back for a second interview shows that the employer has a real interest in the applicant.

Write It, page 99

Your thank-you letter should have two paragraphs. The first paragraph should thank the employer for the interview, restate your interest in the job, and summarize your skills and strengths. The second paragraph should restate your telephone number and invite the employer to call if more information is needed. Compare your finished letter to the sample in the Reference Handbook on page 184. For more information on how to type a professional letter, see the sample on page 182.

Review, page 100

1. "I'm very interested in pursuing a career in landscaping in the future. Right now, I want to work hard to learn all I can about grounds keeping. I've taken a class in agriculture, and I want some practical experience. I have a driver's license and experience driving a truck. I'm good at following directions and promise that I will work hard."

2. Paul is probably concerned that Sadrac will leave the job soon to go back to school. He may also be concerned that Sadrac will move out of the area to go to school. Paul is obviously looking for an employee who plans to stay on the job for a while.

3. Any two of the following. You may have other questions as well.
   - "How would I be trained for this job?"
   - "Are there any opportunities for advancement within the city landscaping department?"
   - "When will you be making a decision?"
   - Other specific questions about the job or the organization that would reflect his research on those areas.

4. Any two of the following: Sadrac should make a record of the interview, noting the name and date of the interview, the name of the interviewer, any required follow up, and other information about the job, organization, or specific questions. He should write a thank-you letter to Paul Garrett. He should call Paul in about a week if he has not heard anything about the job.

PROGRAM 6: READY FOR WORK

Understanding Your Employer's Expectations

WorkSkills, page 107

1. b, e, f, g

2. You may have listed some of these points: Your co-workers are counting on you to be on time. If you are late, others have to do your work for you. Show appreciation to your co-workers for their help in training you. Be friendly with everyone—co-workers, supervisors, and customers—even if you don't like everyone. Do your best to solve problems and work well with others.

WorkSkills, page 109

1. Learning from co-workers is key to your success on the job. You need to work together as a team to get the work done. If you don't get along or if some people do less than their share, anger can result, and the team stops working well together.

2. Show respect by continuing to listen. Ask questions. Follow your co-worker's instructions. Later you can approach the task your way after you gain some experience on the job.

3. (2)

Communicate, page 109

You should have interviewed two people about their first day on the job. You should have asked questions about what problems they faced and how they solved them. You should have also asked for their advice. Your paragraph should summarize the advice you gathered during the two interviews and how you will apply it on the job.

Learning the Meaning of "Work-Ready"

WorkSkills, page 111

1. (4)

2. Kent should show respect for his supervisor by listening carefully and making the changes. He should be open to hearing suggestions and learning new things.

WorkSkills, page 113

1. Melido should wait until he can talk calmly to Nita about the problem. He should not be critical of Nita. Instead, he should work with her to find a solution. If he cannot resolve the problem by talking it out, he should discuss the problem with his supervisor.

2. a, c

Write It, page 113

You should have written a short description of a time when you were faced with a difficult problem and arrived at a solution. Your description of how you solved the problem should demonstrate creativity, persistence, and initiative.

Working as a New Hire

WorkSkills, page 115

1. Any two of the following: Learn their names, be open to learning new things, don't be short-tempered or defensive if you make a mistake, be friendly and professional with everyone, always put in a full day's work, observe your co-workers and adapt to them, don't criticize your co-workers, ask co-workers for their help and advice

2. (2)

3. Seong should remain friendly. Since Seong is new, he doesn't need to defend or criticize the supervisor. He can listen without being drawn into complaining, too.

WorkSkills, page 117

1. Any three of the following: You can develop new work skills, build personal skills, build a work history, and meet people who can help you in the future.

2. You can develop communication and problem-solving skills in every job.

3. (2)

Write It, page 117

Your letter should start with a greeting and end with an appropriate closing. You should have done these things: start with a friendly question asking him how things are going, tell him that you heard he was thinking of quitting his job, give him two or three reasons to stay on the job, and ask him to let you know what he decides to do.

Review, page 118

1. Rachel should make sure that she will get back on time. She can eat lunch with her co-workers and then go back to the workplace before they run their errands. If she does this in a friendly way, her co-workers will understand.

2. Any three of the following: Rachel can be at work on time, work hard, and put in a full day's work. She can be friendly and professional with supervisors, co-workers, and customers. She can have a positive attitude. She can take responsibility for her mistakes and show a willingness to learn. She can show initiative and look for solutions to problems.

3. Rachel could set a goal to continue working while Helen is talking. She could give Helen a friendly smile when she tells jokes, but not encourage her by talking or participating in the office gossip. If the problems continue, Rachel could set a goal to calmly talk to Helen about the problem.

PROGRAM 7: WORKPLACE SAFETY

Understanding Safety Issues

WorkSkills, page 125

1. Any three of the following: An unclean workplace, improperly used or stored cleaning chemicals, poor lighting, unclear pathways, loud sounds, broken furniture, poorly maintained equipment

2. Read the label; read the Material Safety Data Sheet; understand first-aid procedures for the product; put on any necessary protective equipment required by employer, label, or MSDS

3. (4)

WorkSkills, page 127

1. True

2. True

3. True

4. Workers have a responsibility to learn and follow all the employer's safety procedures. The procedures have been developed to avoid accidents. Employers must protect workers from hazards, but workers also need to follow safety procedures to avoid risk.

Write It, page 127

You should have found a product in your home that could be harmful if misused, such as bleach, toilet bowl cleaner, insect or rodent killer, or over-the-counter medicine. After reading the directions and the warning label, you should have written a safety procedure for handling the substance and posted it on the product or near where it is stored.

Recognizing Safety Issues

WorkSkills, page 129

Greg should put on rubber gloves and be sure the area is ventilated. Then he can use water and a mop to clean the spill. If a sewer drain is nearby, he can mop the spill down the drain. Greg should be careful not to allow the CleanJet to touch his skin or splash into his eyes.

WorkSkills, page 131

1. Lee should have washed her hands because germs could be present even though no blood was on the gloves. By not washing her hands, Lee could be spreading one child's germs to herself and other children.

2. (1)

3. Each step in the procedures was developed for a reason—to keep you, your co-workers, and the public healthy and safe. A worker should follow each step even if he or she does not know the reason behind it. For more information, a worker can ask the supervisor the purpose of each step.

Math Matters, page 131

- 1/4 cup of concentrate, 2 cups of water
- 6 fluid ounces concentrate, 48 fluid ounces water
- 2 teaspoons concentrate, 16 teaspoons water

Learning How to Protect Yourself and Your Co-workers

WorkSkills, page 133

1. True
2. True
3. True
4. (2)
5. (4)

WorkSkills, page 135

1. Workers have the responsibility to watch for hazards at the workplace. They must read and understand the safety rules, and they must follow the rules exactly. Workers must also use common sense to keep the workplace safe.

2. (2)

3. This is a hazardous situation. The equipment needs to be evaluated and probably fixed. If you do not report the situation, someone could get a dangerous shock from the equipment.

Communicate, page 135

Your list should include the important points you want to communicate to your friend. For instance, you may want to stress the danger of sleepiness preventing alertness, explain the dangers you foresee, and suggest ways to stay wide-awake and alert.

Review, page 136

1. No people should be standing or moving in the area; the load should be positioned evenly on the pallet; no other vehicles should be moving in the area; he should be aware of other objects in the area; and his seat belts and body restraints should be secured.

2. Any two of the following: His supervisor, experienced co-workers, safety instructions for the forklift.

3. James should never operate the forklift near people or moving objects. He should wait for everyone to leave the loading dock before he begins. If necessary, he should ask them to move away from the area, explaining why.

PROGRAM 8: LEARNING AT WORK

Learning on the Job

WorkSkills, page 143

1. Any three of the following: You can learn from company training programs, from co-workers, by observing the example of others, and by learning how your job fits into the big picture.

2. (4)

3. Any of the following: The training may provide information that Luke needs to do a good job; knowledge about the medicines may help Luke advance in his job.

WorkSkills, page 145

1. (2)

2. Asking questions may be the only way you can find out the information that you need to do your job well. Asking questions can also prevent unnecessary mistakes.

Tech Tip, page 145

Any of the following. You may have written other questions as well.

- "What other companies sell similar <u>products</u> and <u>services</u>?"
- "What are the <u>safety hazards</u> in doing my job?"
- "What are some things I can do to <u>get along</u> well with my <u>co-workers</u>?"
- "Does my company have <u>other stores or offices</u> in the United States?"
- "Are there any <u>training courses</u> for my career on the Internet?"

Note: For each question, you would also need to list your specific career field or company name as part of the search. For example, if you were a masonry worker in the construction field and you wanted to find out about safety hazards, you could search for *safety hazards in masonry and construction.*

Taking Charge of Your Own Training

WorkSkills, page 147

1. False
2. True
3. False
4. You may need to refer to it later on.
5. You are responsible for learning the information that your employer provides. You should quickly review each page of information you are given, prioritize what you need to learn, read urgent items immediately, decide the best time to read any remaining information, and ultimately add all important information to your filing system.

WorkSkills, page 149

1. (3)
2. Feedback can help you understand how your employer views your performance. Feedback can help you make positive changes in your work habits. Seeking feedback shows your employer that you care about the needs of the company.

Write It, page 149

You should have gathered and filled out two forms. Your responses on the forms should be printed neatly in black ink. You should have asked a friend to review your work and give suggestions.

Training over the Long Term

WorkSkills, page 151

1. False
2. True
3. True
4. (3)
5. By assessing your work honestly, you can make improvements in your work before problems arise. Assessing your work also shows your employer that you care about the quality of your work. You can focus your energy on acquiring skills you lack. Plus, you will be better prepared to take advantage of opportunities for advancement.

WorkSkills, page 153

1. The best time to update a resume is right after a new skill is learned. If Helene waits until later, she may forget important details about the training.
2. Any two of the following: You can gain new work skills. You may meet other workers who can help you move up in your career. You can learn to work as part of a team. You also show your employer that you care about the welfare of the company.

Write It, page 153

Your one-year learning plan should contain three to five skills that you want to gain during the year. For each skill, you should have written one or two things that you could do to acquire and practice the skill. You should also have written the date by which you hope to acquire each skill. You should also have posted your plan where you can see it often.

Review, page 154

1. Sandy could seek formal training opportunities, ask a co-worker for help, and observe her co-workers and supervisor selling products to customers.
2. Any three of the following: Sandy could repeat key information back to Eliza Kang to make sure she understands, take notes, practice using what she has learned, and ask Eliza for feedback.
3. Sandy could gain skills that she may need in the future to move up in the company. She could also meet other employees and expand her network of professional contacts. She would show initiative and an eagerness to learn, also increasing her chance of advancement.

Glossary

action verb: a word that plainly tells what someone does, for instance, *build, drive,* and *write*

adaptive skills: personality traits or personal qualities

administrator: a person who manages or is in charge of a business

allowances: numbers that the government uses to figure out how much income tax should be withheld from an employee's paycheck during each pay period

alphabetical: arranged according to the letters of the alphabet

annual wage: the amount of pay an employee earns in one year

applicant: someone who applies for a job

aptitude: ability

assessments: checks or tests that measure how well an employee has accomplished a goal or is performing a task up to a certain standard

background checks: examinations of the facts about an applicant's education and work experiences

benefits: employee sick leave, vacation, and insurance assistance that is paid by the company

body language: communication through hand gestures, posture, and facial expressions

candidate: a person who is seeking a job

career path: a carefully chosen series of jobs within a given profession. A career path usually begins with an entry-level job in a profession. Over time, as an employee gains more knowledge and experience, the career path will include jobs involving more responsibilities and higher pay.

careers: job positions for which a person plans and trains

categories: groups with similar characteristics

challenges: tasks that test the limits of a worker's skills and knowledge

chemicals: substances that are active ingredients in a product. In the workplace, chemicals are usually found in liquids, powders, and gases.

commitment: a pledge or promise to do something

commuting: traveling to and from work

cons: reasons *not* to take a job

conservative clothing: clothes appropriate for the workplace. Conservative clothing is attractive but doesn't stand out in a flashy way.

consumer: someone who buys goods and services

counselor: someone who is trained to give advice about a particular subject

criticism: comments that point out faults. *Constructive criticism* suggests ways to correct faults.

culture: the customs, beliefs, and work styles that characterize a company or work group

discriminate: to make a hiring decision based on some characteristic other than a person's ability to do the job

documents: written or printed papers that contain information

economy: the financial health of a city, state, or country

evaluate: to decide the worth of something

expectations: outcomes that a person hopes will occur. The skills and behaviors an employer hopes to find in employees.

factors: working conditions and facts about a job that influence a job seeker's evaluation of a job

feedback: information that helps a person evaluate how well he or she communicated or performed on a certain occasion, such as a job interview

fixed expenses: amounts that a person knows he or she will have to spend each month

follow up: to take steps to stay in contact with a potential employer after the job interview

formal training: classroom instruction given to employees to provide information or teach a skill

goals: end points a person wants to reach

hazards: possible risks to safety or possible causes of an accident

impression: the feelings someone has about an individual after meeting him or her. The effect someone has on someone else.

incident report: a form that employees must fill out to report an on-the-job accident or injury. Also called an *accident report* or an *injury report.*

initiative: the ability to use positive energy to begin or complete a task

interest: the cost of borrowing money

Internet: a worldwide group of computer networks that have been linked together

inventories: tests or evaluations of related skills and abilities

job: a duty performed regularly by an employee for a specified wage, or payment

job description: a document that explains the duties, responsibilities, and requirements for a particular job title

mandatory: required

Material Safety Data Sheet: (MSDS) a list of information required by law to be provided for each product that contains potentially harmful chemicals

maturity: a state of development associated with being an adult. Mature workers consider the needs of their employer and co-workers as well as their own.

morale: a group's feelings about its responsibilities and challenges

networking: establishing contacts for help and support in the job search

not applicable: abbreviated N/A, a phrase used on a form to show that an item does not apply to the person who filled it out

obligations: actions required by an employer

on-line: being connected to a computer network

open-ended questions: questions that do not have one right answer

outlook: what to expect in the future

overtime pay: wages paid when an employee works extra hours

payroll deductions: money that is withheld from an employee's paycheck

persistence: refusing to give up. Working hard at something until it is achieved.

personnel office: a workplace department that handles hiring and benefits. Often called *human resources department.*

portfolio: a collection of a person's best work

posture: how a person positions his or her body when standing, sitting, or walking

precautions: safety measures taken before a product or machine is used

prerequisite skills: skills you must have before you can do a particular job

priorities: goals put in order according to their importance

prioritize: to decide the order in which to do work tasks, based on their importance or urgency

procedure: a list of steps to be followed to accomplish a task. Safety procedures help reduce the risk of on-the-job accidents and injuries.

proofread: to carefully read a message to find and correct errors

pros: reasons to take a job

protective equipment: safety devices used by workers to reduce the risk of injury when handling chemicals or when using tools and machines. Protective equipment includes goggles, face shields, helmets, rubber gloves, noise protectors, and ear coverings.

punctual: on time

qualifications: accomplishments that make a person well suited for a job

reasonable accommodations: arrangements or equipment needed to enable a special-needs individual to do a job, such as a large-type computer keyboard for the sight-impaired

recommendation: a statement about a worker's skills and attitude

references: people who know an applicant well and can talk about his or her work habits and skills

regulations: government rules that are designed to protect people. Safety regulations ensure that companies take measures to keep their workers safe.

repetitive motion injuries: physical problems that are caused by repeating the same movement for a long period of time

requirements: skills and experiences needed to do a certain job. Skills, training, or conditions that an employer requires.

resume: a short summary of a job applicant's skills and experiences

routine: actions that are done regularly

screen out: to reject a job applicant before the interview stage

sick leave: an amount of time that an employee is allowed to miss work for reasons of illness without losing pay

skills summary: on a resume, a brief statement summarizing a person's skills and goals

standard of living: a level of comfort measured by what a person owns and earns

temporary job: a job that lasts for a limited time

tone: the attitude and emotions an individual communicates in his or her choice of words and in the sound of his or her voice

transferable skills: skills that can be used on any job

ventilation: fresh air. Ventilation can be improved by opening a window or turning on a fan.

verify: to make sure information is true

vocational colleges: schools that teach practical skills in certain trades

volunteer work: work or a service that is done by someone who does not receive pay

work environment: the surroundings and conditions in which employees do their job

Index

Reference Handbook

Information Worksheet

You will need this information to fill out job application and other employment forms.
Take this information with you to all interviews.

Personal Information

NAME	
ADDRESS	
CITY, STATE, ZIP	

PHONE NUMBERS	(DAYTIME)	(EVENING)	(MESSAGE)

SOCIAL SECURITY NUMBER	DRIVER'S LICENSE NUMBER

Work History (List most recent first. You may list volunteer activities as well.)

JOB 1	JOB TITLE	COMPANY NAME
START DATE	END DATE	COMPANY ADDRESS
ENDING SALARY	SUPERVISOR	PHONE NUMBER

JOB 2	JOB TITLE	COMPANY NAME
START DATE	END DATE	COMPANY ADDRESS
ENDING SALARY	SUPERVISOR	PHONE NUMBER

JOB 3	JOB TITLE	COMPANY NAME
START DATE	END DATE	COMPANY ADDRESS
ENDING SALARY	SUPERVISOR	PHONE NUMBER

JOB 4	JOB TITLE	COMPANY NAME
START DATE	END DATE	COMPANY ADDRESS
ENDING SALARY	SUPERVISOR	PHONE NUMBER

Educational History (List most recent first.)

START DATE	END DATE	SCHOOL
SCHOOL PHONE NUMBER		SCHOOL ADDRESS
CERTIFICATES, DEGREES EARNED		COURSES

START DATE	END DATE	SCHOOL
SCHOOL PHONE NUMBER		SCHOOL ADDRESS
CERTIFICATES, DEGREES EARNED		COURSES

START DATE	END DATE	SCHOOL
SCHOOL PHONE NUMBER		SCHOOL ADDRESS
CERTIFICATES, DEGREES EARNED		COURSES

Sample Resume 1

SAMANTHA L. CASTRO

---

713 W. Broadway Avenue
San Jose, CA 95125
(408) 555-8427

JOB OBJECTIVE

Seeking a challenging general office position with opportunities for professional growth.

EXPERIENCE

Copy Clerk
Los Angeles Herald, Los Angeles, CA   May 1995 to Present
Duties: Distribute newspapers and mail daily to company departments. Assist with
            photocopying and fax. Run errands and handle light typing duties. Fill in for
            receptionist as needed.

Service Writer
Jennings Automotive, San Jose, CA   Jan. 1994 to May 1995
Duties: Wrote up customer orders and invoices. Assigned jobs to appropriate departments
            and followed jobs through to completion. Handled customer telephone inquiries
            and customer complaints.

Sales Clerk
$5 Sav-Lots Club, Gilroy, CA   Sept. 1992 to Nov. 1993
Duties: Assisted customers in the linen department with purchases and prices. Substituted in other
            departments as needed. Acted as relief cashier. Kept the department clean and orderly.

SKILLS

Typing–40 words per minute
Ten-Key–120 strokes per minute
Software–Windows 3.1 and 95, Microsoft WORD and EXCEL
Bilingual–Spanish and English
Business Machines–Fax, copier, scanner, computer, word processor,
and multi-line business telephone system.

EDUCATION

Hancock Park High School, Los Angeles, CA   Graduated: May 1992
Courses: Bookkeeping, Business Writing, Office Procedures, Word Processing

---

REFERENCES AVAILABLE UPON REQUEST

Sample Resume 2

Julian Harris
975 Point View Drive
Clarksville, TN 37042
(615) 555-2144

Job Summary   Seeking a job in the construction trades in which I can use my carpentry skills and develop new skills.

Work History   *Handyman*   June 1997 to the present
ACE Home Repair   Clarksville, TN
Work at homes as assigned. Paint inside and outside walls. Clear trash and debris. Repair fences and gates. Small plumbing repairs. Replace screens and install storm windows.

Carpenter's Helper   August 1995 to May 1997
Lincoln Construction   Madisonville, KY
Installed window frames, door frames, doors, weather stripping, trim, and hardware. Loaded materials on truck. Some experience installing paneling and laying floors.

Cannery Line Worker   March 1995 to August 1995
Hickman Meats   Madisonville, KY
Part-time job while finishing high school. Sorted meat into processing machines. Inspected products on the line.

Skills   Good at following directions and reading blueprints. Good at solving math problems and using measurements. Eager to learn new skills.

Education   *Associate Degree in the Construction Trades*   September 1995 to June 1997
Madisonville Community College   Madisonville, KY
General coursework in all aspects of the construction trades with an emphasis on Carpentry and Woodworking.

High School Degree   June 1995
Madisonville High School   Madisonville, KY
Completed woodshop and advanced woodworking.

References Available Upon Request

How to Type a Business Letter

The letters you send to an employer are samples of your work. Make sure your letters are neatly typed and error free. If you do the work on a computer or word processor, you can easily make corrections. Use the following spacing to produce professional-looking documents.

MARGINS

- Leave a top margin of $1\frac{1}{2}$ to 2 inches, or 9 to 12 blank lines.
- Leave a bottom margin of at least 1 inch, or 6 blank lines.
- Set the side margins at 1 or $1\frac{1}{2}$ inches.

HEADING

- Start typing at the very left of the page.
- Type the date on about the twelfth blank line.
- Leave one blank line.
- Type the return address (your address).
- Leave three blank lines.
- Type the name and address of the person to whom you are writing.

OPENING

- Leave one blank line.
- Type "Dear" and the name of the person to whom you are writing, followed by a colon.

BODY

- Leave one blank line between paragraphs.

CLOSING

- Type "Sincerely" followed by a comma.
- Leave four blank lines and type your name.
- If you are enclosing a resume, leave one blank line and type the word *Enclosure*.
- Sign the letter in black ink.

Spacing Guide

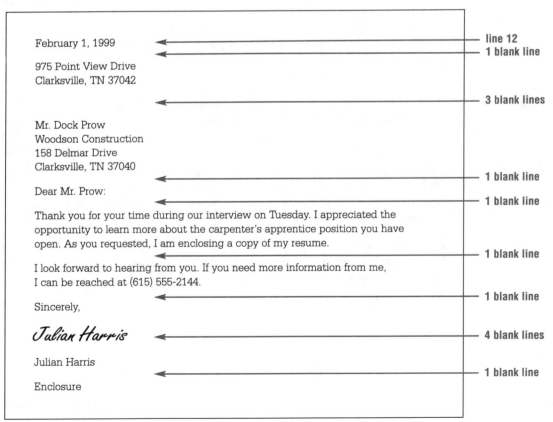

February 1, 1999 — line 12 / 1 blank line

975 Point View Drive
Clarksville, TN 37042 — 3 blank lines

Mr. Dock Prow
Woodson Construction
158 Delmar Drive
Clarksville, TN 37040 — 1 blank line

Dear Mr. Prow: — 1 blank line

Thank you for your time during our interview on Tuesday. I appreciated the opportunity to learn more about the carpenter's apprentice position you have open. As you requested, I am enclosing a copy of my resume. — 1 blank line

I look forward to hearing from you. If you need more information from me, I can be reached at (615) 555-2144. — 1 blank line

Sincerely,

Julian Harris — 4 blank lines

Julian Harris — 1 blank line

Enclosure

Sample Cover Letter

Whenever you send a resume through the mail, you should write a cover letter to go with it. Put the cover letter on top of the resume so that the employer will see it first. Do not staple it to your resume.

Type your letter carefully; see "How to Type a Business Letter" on page 182 of this Reference Handbook. A good cover letter has three paragraphs:

- The first paragraph explains why you are sending your resume.
- The second paragraph introduces you. It gives the employer a preview of your skills and strengths.
- The third paragraph makes a request. Usually, you will be asking for an interview.

January 22, 1999

713 W. Broadway Avenue
San Jose, CA 95125

Robin Roberts
Pacific Bank
405 S. Fairfax Avenue
San Jose, CA 95113

Dear Ms. Roberts:

I am writing to apply for the office assistant job that you advertised in the *Los Angeles Times* on Tuesday, January 20, 1999.

I type 40 words per minute, and I am familiar with both word processing and spreadsheet software. In my job as a Copy Clerk at the offices of the *Herald*, I had the opportunity to learn a variety of office skills, including many computer skills. In addition, I have experience filling out forms and keeping records. I am fluent in both speaking and writing Spanish.

I am enclosing my resume and would like the opportunity to meet with you to discuss my qualifications for the position you have available. I will call you on Monday to schedule an appointment, or you can reach me at (408) 555-8427. Thank you for your consideration.

Sincerely,

Samantha L. Castro

Samantha L. Castro

Enclosure

Sample Thank-You Letter

Follow up information and job interviews with a thank-you letter. Type the letter as you would any business letter. See "How to Type a Business Letter" on page 182 of this Reference Handbook.

In a thank-you letter:
- Thank the employer for the interview.
- Review one or two points about your skills.
- Tell the employer how to get in touch with you.

Here is a model for the body of a thank-you letter.

Thank you for taking the time on Monday to interview me for the position of Office Assistant. I enjoyed learning more about your company and the requirements of the job.

After learning more about the position, I feel confident that I could provide the help you need. I am a hard worker and I enjoy challenges. I understand the importance of being on time and putting in a full day's work. I hope you will give me the chance to work at Pacific Bank.

If you need more information, please call me at (408) 555-8427. I look forward to hearing from you.

Preparing a List of References

Your list of references should be neatly typed on a standard-size sheet of paper. List each reference's name, job title, address, and phone number. Your reference list may look something like the model below.

SAMANTHA L. CASTRO

713 W. Broadway Avenue
San Jose, CA 95125
(408) 555-8427

REFERENCES

Patricia Goldhamer, Supervisor of Copy Desk
Los Angeles Herald
1361 W. Venice Boulevard, Los Angeles, CA 90006
(213) 555-9307 Extension 1339

Nick Davidson, Director of Volunteers
Los Angeles Community Center
201 N. Gardner Avenue, Los Angeles, CA 90048
(213) 555-1326

Sandy Logan, Instructor
Hancock Park High School
607 N. Crestview Drive, Los Angeles, CA 90036
(213) 555-6184